STAR WARS
THE LAST JEDI
THE VISUAL DICTIONARY

Stereoscopic vision helps in spotting fish

Dense feathers and down insulate body

Webbed rear-set feet ideal for swimming

PORG

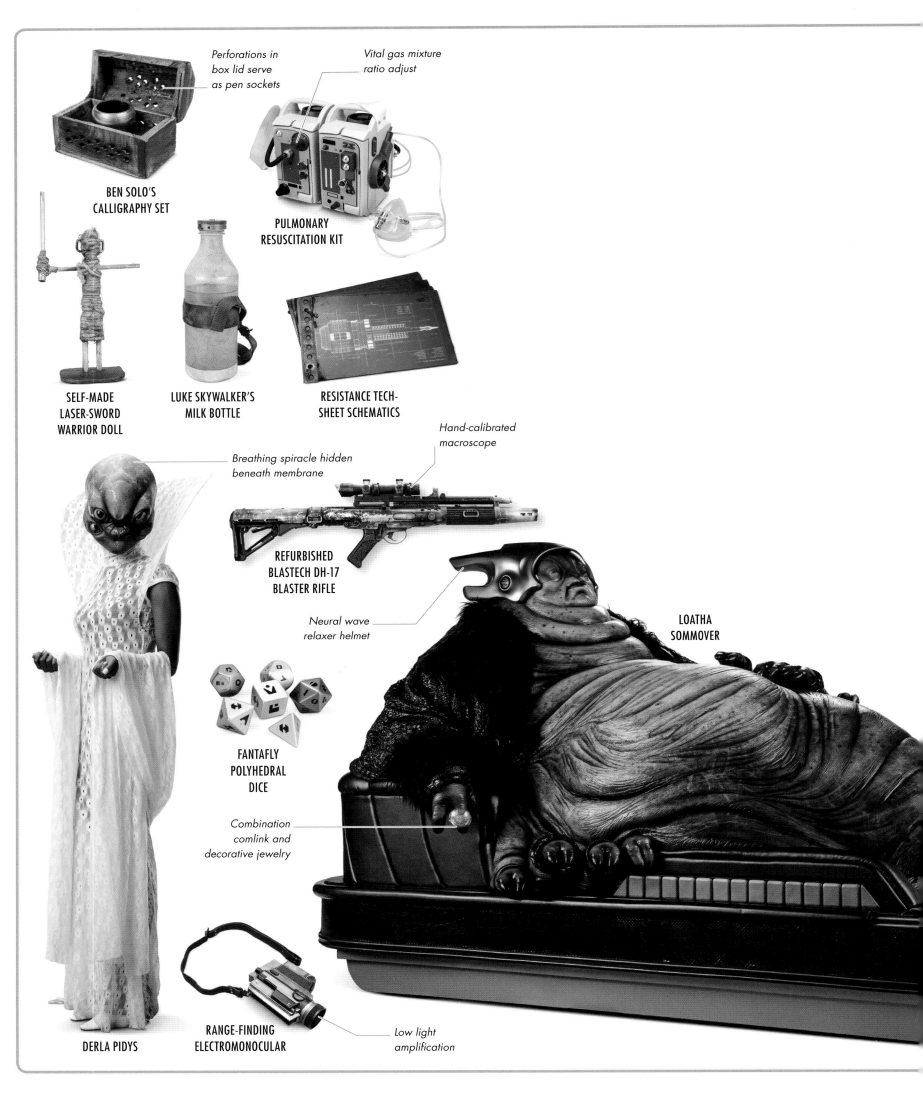

Perforations in box lid serve as pen sockets

BEN SOLO'S CALLIGRAPHY SET

Vital gas mixture ratio adjust

PULMONARY RESUSCITATION KIT

SELF-MADE LASER-SWORD WARRIOR DOLL

LUKE SKYWALKER'S MILK BOTTLE

RESISTANCE TECH-SHEET SCHEMATICS

Breathing spiracle hidden beneath membrane

Hand-calibrated macroscope

REFURBISHED BLASTECH DH-17 BLASTER RIFLE

Neural wave relaxer helmet

LOATHA SOMMOVER

FANTAFLY POLYHEDRAL DICE

Combination comlink and decorative jewelry

DERLA PIDYS

RANGE-FINDING ELECTROMONOCULAR

Low light amplification

STAR WARS
THE LAST JEDI™
THE VISUAL DICTIONARY

GLOWEN FAQUIDDE

WRITTEN BY PABLO HIDALGO

CONTENTS

INTRODUCTION

STAR WARS: THE LAST JEDI returns audiences to the new era
of storytelling that began so spectacularly in *The Force Awakens*.
In true serial fashion, like the films that so heavily inspired the
creation of *Star Wars*, it quite literally picks up where the last chapter
left off. Moviegoers have waited years to learn the further adventures
of Rey, Finn, Poe, and Kylo, but the characters themselves are mere
moments from the events that indelibly shaped them in the last film.
Episode VIII not only propels them on to new challenges and
discoveries, it also unearths secrets from the past.

In this Visual Dictionary, you will visit new worlds, from opulent Cantonica
to desolate Crait. Learn more about secretive characters like Luke
Skywalker and Supreme Leader Snoke. Explore the very birthplace of
the Jedi, an island that also threatens to be the Order's grave. As *The Last
Jedi* provides answers and raises new questions, so too will this book.

STARKILLER AFTERSHOCKS

IT WAS THE CATACLYSM heard around the galaxy. The Starkiller's blast tore the very fabric of hyperspace, and moments later the Hosnian system was no more. With a single shot, the First Order decapitated the New Republic, and across the galaxy worlds began to surrender. Many were already leaning toward the First Order's promise of security. Others were terrified into capitulation. In the span of only a few days, the galactic status quo was irrevocably upset, and a long-simmering cold war burst into flames.

THE NEW REPUBLIC

Despite its idealistic intentions, the New Republic never took root on a scale comparable to the Old Republic. Now the Senate and fleet are gone, along with the Republic's top military commanders, and it seems unlikely that the remaining systems will be able to hold together, let alone hold off the First Order.

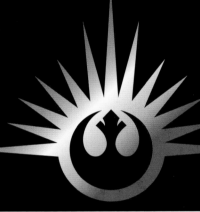

THE FIRST ORDER

Although Starkiller Base has been destroyed, the First Order is not wallowing in defeat. Instead, it believes the war is as good as won. All that remains is to mop up the last survivors of the Resistance, hunt down and destroy Luke Skywalker, and then claim victory over a galaxy still reeling from the First Order's sneak attack.

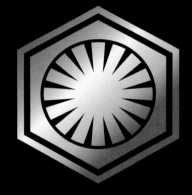

THE RESISTANCE

The Resistance's primary objective had always been to spur the Senate into action against the First Order. That is no longer possible, and the Resistance finds its options are limited. General Organa knows that a single victory does not win a war, and right now the priority for the Resistance is escape, so that it can live to fight another day.

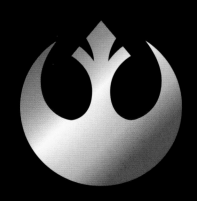

THE GALAXY

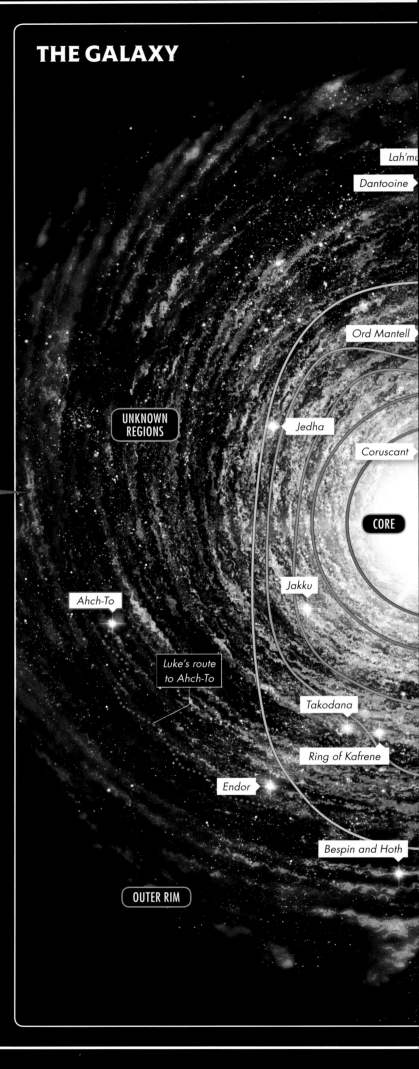

Lah'mu

Dantooine

Ord Mantell

UNKNOWN REGIONS

Jedha

Coruscant

CORE

Jakku

Ahch-To

Luke's route to Ahch-To

Takodana

Ring of Kafrene

Endor

Bespin and Hoth

OUTER RIM

THE HOSNIAN CATACLYSM

The atomization of the New Republic's capital and home fleet led to the immediate surrender of many worlds to the First Order. It was a stark demonstration of peerless power, and of the First Order's willingness to commit mass murder without hesitation.

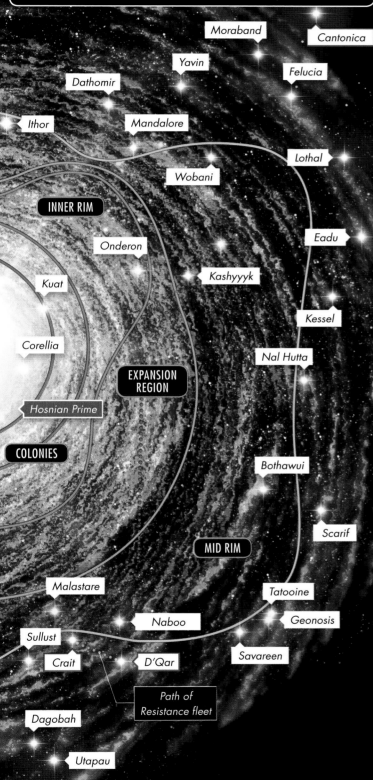

Moraband

Cantonica

Yavin

Felucia

Dathomir

Ithor

Mandalore

Lothal

Wobani

INNER RIM

Eadu

Onderon

Kashyyyk

Kuat

Kessel

Corellia

Nal Hutta

EXPANSION REGION

Hosnian Prime

Bothawui

COLONIES

Scarif

MID RIM

Malastare

Tatooine

Naboo

Geonosis

Sullust

Crait

D'Qar

Savareen

Path of Resistance fleet

Dagobah

Utapau

D'QAR

A First Order counterattack is inevitable. Immediately after the departure of Rey aboard the *Millennium Falcon*, the Resistance begins evacuating its stronghold on the verdant world of D'Qar. Lieutenant Connix leads the evacuation effort, loading Resistance personnel and equipment aboard emergency transports as quickly as possible. The Resistance fleet, having only just arrived following the distress call dispatched during the Starkiller battle, hovers above the planet in low orbit, the ships rapidly filling up their hangar bays with emergency transports.

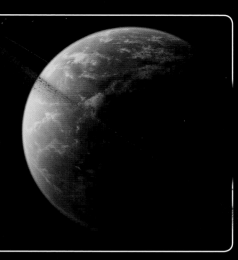

AHCH-TO

An uncharted world whose location in the galaxy was lost in antiquity, Ahch-To was known by many names in ancient legends, which only further confounded attempts to find it. Orbiting twin suns, the planet is mostly covered in oceans, with scattered archipelagos dotting the restless waters. It is the world where the Jedi Order was founded, and was the site of the first Jedi temple. After decades of searching, Luke Skywalker unlocked the mystery of its location, and voyaged here. Ahch-To is no paradise, however. It is a world of salt spray, cold winds, and violent storms.

CANTONICA

Located within the distant Corporate Sector of space—a fiefdom where corporate entities are given free rein to govern their own territory—the planet Cantonica is a symbol of wealth and luxury. It is naturally a desolate, desert world, but huge sums of money have been spent on a vast infrastructure that has transformed one section of its landscape into an artificial seaside city: Canto Bight. This opulent resort is the playground for the galaxy's super rich, who have enough power and influence to remain untouched by the rapidly expanding war.

CRAIT

A remote mineral world, Crait was initially scouted by Bail Organa as a potential rebel outpost during the early days of the Rebellion. A 16-year-old Leia Organa visited Crait, and saw firsthand how empty and uninviting a wasteland it appeared to be—the ideal place for a rebel refuge. It is a world of blood-red crystal, dusted by a permanent coating of blinding-white salt. The remains of an old mine became the foundation of a Rebel Alliance outpost; decades after the war against the Empire ended, the base lies empty and abandoned.

RESISTANCE FLEET

WITH ONLY FOUR SHIPS, the Resistance effort to evacuate D'Qar barely qualifies as a fleet—and yet this ragtag assembly of transports and cruisers is vital for rescuing the doomed base's personnel. Reinforcements take the form of bombers, additional X-wing fighters, and A-wing interceptors, as well as seasoned commanders. Lifeboats quickly ferry people from the planet's surface to the waiting ships, trying to escape the inevitable First Order reprisal. Just as the last transport departs D'Qar, the First Order launches an orbital bombardment.

The engineering depths of the capital ships soon teem with evacuees, as sections usually reserved for maintenance workers are hastily repurposed to accommodate the influx of extra crew.

THE *RADDUS*

Stretching over three kilometers in length, the enormous *Raddus* is General Organa's flagship, and was one of the last warships designed prior to the disarmament treaty between the New Republic and defeated Empire. The heavy cruiser served in the New Republic home fleet for a time, but was retired in favor of a less crew-intensive design. Increased automation and the removal of redundant systems have made the cruiser a viable Resistance asset. The *Raddus*' key strength is its advanced deflector shield system that can push the envelope of protective energy far from its hull.

Comms antenna

Midship turbolaser battery blister

Primary command bridge

Aft section enveloped by intensified deflector screens

Starboard hangar bay

Insulated ground crew headset

Borrowed starfighter pilot helmet

FLEET CREWS

The Resistance is so understaffed that the D'Qar base personnel change roles to be of better service aboard the capital ships. Communications techs become evacuation shuttle pilots, medics work as mechanics, and armorers become gunners as needed. Duty officers on the capital ships implement emergency plans for the intake of evacuees and reassign them to key roles on their respective vessels. Personnel from scattered cells must suddenly work side by side, forging strong new relationships in the face of the newest First Order threat. The *Raddus* takes the bulk of Leia's unit, with spillover to the *Anodyne*, the *Ninka*, and the *Vigil* in that order.

PAMMICH NERRO GOODE, TRANSPORT PILOT

Holstered Glie-44 blaster pistol

SAILE MINNAU, GUARD

RIVA ROSETTA, TECHNICIAN

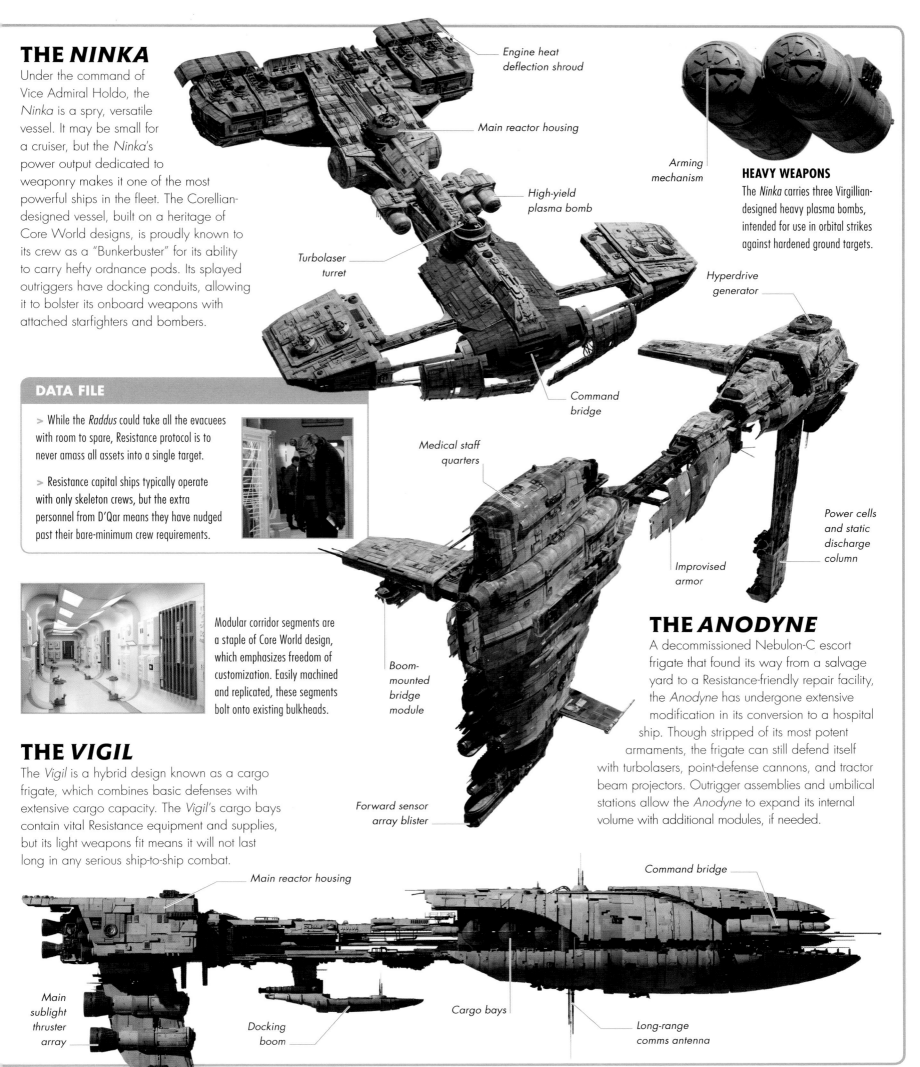

THE *NINKA*

Under the command of Vice Admiral Holdo, the *Ninka* is a spry, versatile vessel. It may be small for a cruiser, but the *Ninka*'s power output dedicated to weaponry makes it one of the most powerful ships in the fleet. The Corellian-designed vessel, built on a heritage of Core World designs, is proudly known to its crew as a "Bunkerbuster" for its ability to carry hefty ordnance pods. Its splayed outriggers have docking conduits, allowing it to bolster its onboard weapons with attached starfighters and bombers.

Engine heat deflection shroud

Main reactor housing

High-yield plasma bomb

Turbolaser turret

Arming mechanism

HEAVY WEAPONS
The *Ninka* carries three Virgillian-designed heavy plasma bombs, intended for use in orbital strikes against hardened ground targets.

Command bridge

Hyperdrive generator

DATA FILE

> While the *Raddus* could take all the evacuees with room to spare, Resistance protocol is to never amass all assets into a single target.

> Resistance capital ships typically operate with only skeleton crews, but the extra personnel from D'Qar means they have nudged past their bare-minimum crew requirements.

Medical staff quarters

Improvised armor

Power cells and static discharge column

Modular corridor segments are a staple of Core World design, which emphasizes freedom of customization. Easily machined and replicated, these segments bolt onto existing bulkheads.

Boom-mounted bridge module

THE *ANODYNE*

A decommissioned Nebulon-C escort frigate that found its way from a salvage yard to a Resistance-friendly repair facility, the *Anodyne* has undergone extensive modification in its conversion to a hospital ship. Though stripped of its most potent armaments, the frigate can still defend itself with turbolasers, point-defense cannons, and tractor beam projectors. Outrigger assemblies and umbilical stations allow the *Anodyne* to expand its internal volume with additional modules, if needed.

THE *VIGIL*

The *Vigil* is a hybrid design known as a cargo frigate, which combines basic defenses with extensive cargo capacity. The *Vigil*'s cargo bays contain vital Resistance equipment and supplies, but its light weapons fit means it will not last long in any serious ship-to-ship combat.

Forward sensor array blister

Main reactor housing

Command bridge

Main sublight thruster array

Docking boom

Cargo bays

Long-range comms antenna

FLEET COMMAND

THE HIGH COMMAND of the Resistance fleet comprises a mixture of Alliance veterans, ex-leaders of independent defense forces, and New Republic converts—all of whom share a personal connection to General Organa. With lessons learned from the Rebellion, the command structure of the fleet is extremely flexible: The command crews aboard the ships that arrive to evacuate D'Qar are combined with the officers directly under Leia's command. Emergency plans are set in motion, but no one is truly prepared for the ferocity of the First Order assault.

LIEUTENANT CONNIX

Kaydel Connix of Dulathia earns a promotion to lieutenant for her admirable service as an operations controller during the Starkiller crisis—and from the necessity of having an officer lead the D'Qar evacuation. Her word is the ultimate authority when it comes to prioritizing and carrying out an orderly retreat. Once aboard the *Raddus*, she returns to her sensor ops position but retains her rank.

Army lieutenant's rank badge

Rigid mantle made of cartilage

Gular sac with feeler tendrils

Admiral's rank badge

The *Raddus* bridge crew consists of human and Mon Calamari officers younger than Ackbar—in some case, by many decades. The gruff admiral often refers to them as "fry."

Battle analysis computer (BAC) data-feed

RESISTANCE MDS-440 DATAPAD

ADMIRAL ACKBAR

With the *Raddus'* arrival at D'Qar, Admiral Ackbar retakes his command chair within the heavy cruiser's bridge. Ackbar was a contemporary of the cruiser's namesake—Admiral Raddus—and often clashed with him, as Ackbar's style was more methodical compared to Raddus' improvisational and aggressive nature. With decades of reflection, Ackbar has come to better respect his predecessor, and it was Ackbar who petitioned that the cruiser carry Raddus' name.

CAPTAIN IDROSEN GAWAT

Before his retirement, Gawat led the planetary defense forces that patrolled space in the Mykapo system. Not wanting to hang up his rank badge just yet, he joined the Resistance in his seventies so that his decades of experience could be put to good use.

Brismoss-fiber uniform tunic

Fleet officer's uniform trousers

Service boots

LIEUTENANT GUILA ANGIRA

COMMAND BRIDGE

The *Raddus* has two bridges—a primary command bridge on its upper surface and a secondary battle bridge beneath its prow. When the command bridge is destroyed, operations move to the battle bridge.

Dexterous hands with adhesive fingerpads

Inventory datapad

BOLLIE PRINDEL

An amphibious Urodel, Bollie Prindel is a towering, gentle presence in Resistance command centers. On D'Qar and later the *Raddus*, he serves as quartermaster and inventory officer, tracking the Resistance's steadily dwindling supplies.

BRIDGE CREW

Aboard the *Raddus*, the supreme commander of the Resistance is General Organa, with Admiral Ackbar serving as the ship's commanding officer and overall fleet commander. Executive officer is Captain Gawat; Commander Sesfan heads engineering; Lieutenant Guila Angira, gunnery; Lieutenant Connix, communications and sensors, and Bollie Prindel, supplies. The crew is reshuffled following severe battle damage to the *Raddus*.

OPERATIONS ROOM

The command bridge includes a spacious operations room lined with status boards that track the evolution of battles. A modern command console uses free-floating holograms generated from realtime sensor data, offering a live view of the combat zone. The room is later blasted apart and charred by a First Order missile strike.

FINN

FINN'S REPUTATION is spreading through the Resistance. As the only stormtrooper known to have broken free from the lifelong conditioning and training of the First Order, he is regarded with admiration and curiosity in equal measure. Although he is being praised as a hero, it's a description he does not feel applies. All that is driving Finn at the moment is a longing to ensure Rey's safety. The last thing he recalls seeing before being plunged into unconsciousness was Rey being threatened by Kylo Ren. First Order training psyche-logs, not allowing for such deep personal loyalties, would clinically describe Finn's behavior as "imprinting." He knows it to be something deeper.

Finn stirs from a deep sleep within his medical cocoon. Doctor Harter Kalonia has placed Finn in a medically induced coma, allowing his body to heal free from the mental stress of the emergency evacuation.

RECOVERING WARRIOR

In the rush to leave D'Qar, medics put Finn into an emergency suit filled with healing bacta and deliver him to a temporary medical suite aboard the Resistance flagship, *Raddus*. Finn dozes through the jump to hyperspace, unaware of the relentless First Order pursuit. When he does awaken, his first word is a shouted "REY!," for in his disoriented state, he believes himself to be in the forests of Starkiller Base. Finn groggily staggers out of the medical suite, leaking synthetic bacta, looking for answers in general and Rey in particular.

Finn, stabilized, recovers in a converted storage room lined with portable medical gear. The ship's dedicated medical bay is currently at full capacity tending to injuries sustained in the evacuation.

Flexpoly bacta suit is past its expiration date, making it more fragile

Retaining collar lined by status sensors with wireless telemetry

Synthetic bacta circulation and filtration tubing

Stowed blaster rifle

FINN'S SCOUT BACKPACK

Environmental sensor suite

RUSH TO ACTION

Impulsive Finn rarely plans more than a few steps ahead. On awakening, his first instinct is to find and help Rey. But this brings him into collision with Rose Tico, a maintenance worker standing guard over the *Raddus'* escape pod bay. The pair seem unlikely allies, but Rose's methodical, technical mind coupled with Finn's drive and knowledge of First Order methods allows them to hatch a daring plan—one that will allow the Resistance to shake off the enemy pursuit.

In a gesture of friendship, Poe Dameron repaired Finn's jacket while he recovered

Adjustment dial

SHUTTLE HEADSET

Vo-pickup

Resistance-issue belt

On the salt flats of Crait, Finn puts his speeder training to good use, joining Poe Dameron in an attack on the First Order's invasion force. It is a reckless assault against insurmountable odds, and Finn knows that his chances of survival are small.

Stormtrooper temperature-control body glove

Reactant gas port cap

Power cartridge

Weatherproof adventurer boots

FINN'S BLASTER PISTOL

Finn's lifetime of combat training makes him adept with a wide variety of small arms, well beyond the standard-issue weaponry of the First Order. The rugged Glie-44 pistol is the standard Resistance blaster, and is found in military, police, and civilian holsters the galaxy over.

GENERAL ORGANA

Alderaanian mourning braid

LEIA ORGANA'S TENACITY continues to serve as an inspirational beacon in such dark times. The destruction of the Starkiller was a gasp of victory, but the crushing weight of the First Order advance soon strangles it. The New Republic is in shambles, independent systems are capitulating, and Han Solo has been murdered by her son—this would be enough to crush any lesser being in an avalanche of despair. But like a diamond, Leia shines under such pressure. She knows others look to her for leadership, but this reliance comes with a risk. Leia looks to the future and wonders if the next generation of heroes is ready to take on the mantle of responsibilities once she is gone.

Muted somber colors reflect gravity of situation

Having grown up amid intrigue, and taught well by her adoptive parents, Leia is skilled at keeping secrets. The early Rebellion survived by carefully restricting information on a need-to-know basis. Leia keeps her plans for the survival of the Resistance close.

HOMING BEACON

Leia wears a compact S-thread transmitter bracelet, with Rey holding the mated pair. In this way, Rey will be able to find the ever-mobile Resistance fleet once she recovers Luke Skywalker.

MOST DESPERATE HOUR

The First Order attack on the *Raddus* results in the destruction of the ship's primary command deck. The bridge crew suffers horrendous casualties, and Leia Organa is incapacitated by exposure to the vacuum of space. Medical droids rush to Leia's aid, and soon a battery of devices carefully monitors her life signs as she recuperates. For many in the Resistance, including the officers and soldiers personally recruited by Leia, her absence is the biggest blow to morale they have yet faced.

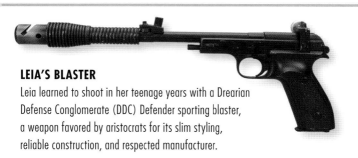

LEIA'S BLASTER

Leia learned to shoot in her teenage years with a Drearian Defense Conglomerate (DDC) Defender sporting blaster, a weapon favored by aristocrats for its slim styling, reliable construction, and respected manufacturer.

ORO-WEAVE BRACELET

SIGNET RINGS

AURODIUM EARRINGS

Leia knows better than to trust that escape into hyperspace will save the Resistance fleet. The power of the Starkiller showed that the First Order wields technology beyond anything she has ever encountered.

C-3PO

Once again C-3PO is caught up in a war where his knowledge of protocol has limited use, leaving him hopelessly out of his programmed depths. Though he found some utility coordinating the activity of Resistance spy droids across the galaxy, the urgent task of moving the Resistance fleet out of reach of the First Order has little need for his skills. Beyond his impeccable language and etiquette abilities, however, C-3PO possesses strong loyalty to Leia Organa, having served her for decades.

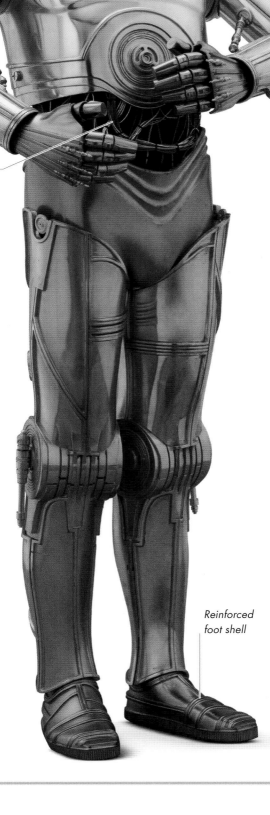

Olfactory sensor

Non-threatening face

Modular appendage socket

MD-15C MEDICAL DROID

Life-signs monitoring system

Multi-system connection wires

REPULSOR GURNEY

With the command structure aboard the *Raddus* constantly shifting, C-3PO scans his databanks for proper succession protocols in an effort to be useful. The closest he can find are recommendations for seating order at the captain's table during formal dinners.

Reinforced foot shell

Lockable power switch

EMERGENCY LIFE-SUPPORT UNIT

POE DAMERON

ANY ACCOLADES bestowed upon Poe for the destruction of Starkiller Base shine only briefly, for the Resistance immediately begins its full-scale evacuation. Emboldened by his victory, Poe brings the fight directly to the First Order fleet—much to the annoyance of General Organa, who frets about Poe's lack of restraint. Buying time and cover for the Resistance bomber squadrons scrambling to hold off the First Order bombardment, Poe takes aim at General Hux's pride, disrespecting him by deliberately mispronouncing Hux's name in a broad-frequency address to both fleets.

Visor in retracted position

SQUADRON LEADER FLIGHT HELMET

Poe's instincts are to keep moving, and he is never at ease when the pace of events slows. The harried evacuation of D'Qar is a real test for Poe, but it is the biding of time that follows the retreat that truly wears at his resolve.

Classic Alliance "starbird" crest

Visor-retaining cowl

Incom-FreiTek 5L5 fusial thrust engine

Retractable anti-glare visor

S-foils in attack position

Accelerator pod

Vo-pickup comm unit

BLACK ONE

Resistance technicians have attached a temporary accelerator pod to the tail of Poe's customized T-70 X-wing fighter. This boosts the fighter's sublight speed so it can zip past First Order point-defense cannons.

Emergency beacon activation switch

GIFTED BUT RECKLESS

General Organa has carefully parceled out duties to Poe. With each success, he is given greater responsibilities, but his ego and recklessness have also grown. This concerns Leia, because for the Resistance to continue, it will need a new generation of leadership to succeed her. Poe respects Leia deeply, and it would hurt him to know that she harbors such doubts.

Insulated, vac-sealable flight suit

Poe loses his beloved *Black One* when it is struck by torpedoes fired by Kylo Ren's TIE silencer. Poe and BB-8 barely survive the explosion.

When an officer is named to carry on the retreat in Leia's absence, Poe is both relieved that it is not him and angered that it is Vice Admiral Holdo. Poe cannot imagine anyone living up to Leia, and finds Holdo's strategy and manner uninspiring. Against protocol, he questions Holdo's orders, stoking insubordination with the same fiery, rebellious demeanor that serves him well in combat.

Rebel Alliance/ Resistance crest

Runyip-leather jacket

RELUCTANT LEADER

Unable to bear Vice Admiral Holdo's secretive and off-putting command style, Poe takes matters into his own hands and conspires against her. Dameron builds a resistance *within* the Resistance, turning to allies like Finn, Rose Tico, Kaydel Connix, and even a reluctant C-3PO. Poe dispatches Finn and Rose to Cantonica on a secret mission to thwart the First Order's hyperspace tracker, all the while trying to uncover just what Holdo is keeping from him.

For his flagrant disregard of her direct orders, General Organa demotes Poe from wing commander to squadron captain. This comes at a time when the Resistance chain of command is becoming increasingly frayed.

Short-range receiver

EARPIECE COMM

Brushed steel washer from rebel tech

RING NECKLACE
Poe wears the wedding ring of his late mother, Shara Bey, on a necklace, waiting to share it someday with the right partner.

DATA FILE

> Most of the surviving pilots who joined Poe in the fight against the Starkiller have since scattered to other evacuation points, or been assigned to other missions.

> The hurried pace of evacuation means Poe has not been properly introduced to Rey.

SPEEDER HEADSET
Poe is confident behind the controls of almost any vehicle, be it a cutting edge starfighter or decrepit repulsorcraft. When the Resistance survivors are forced to make do with aging ski speeders left abandoned on Crait, Poe once again assumes the role of wing commander, regardless of the rank badge he wears.

Holstered Glie-44 blaster pistol (set to stun)

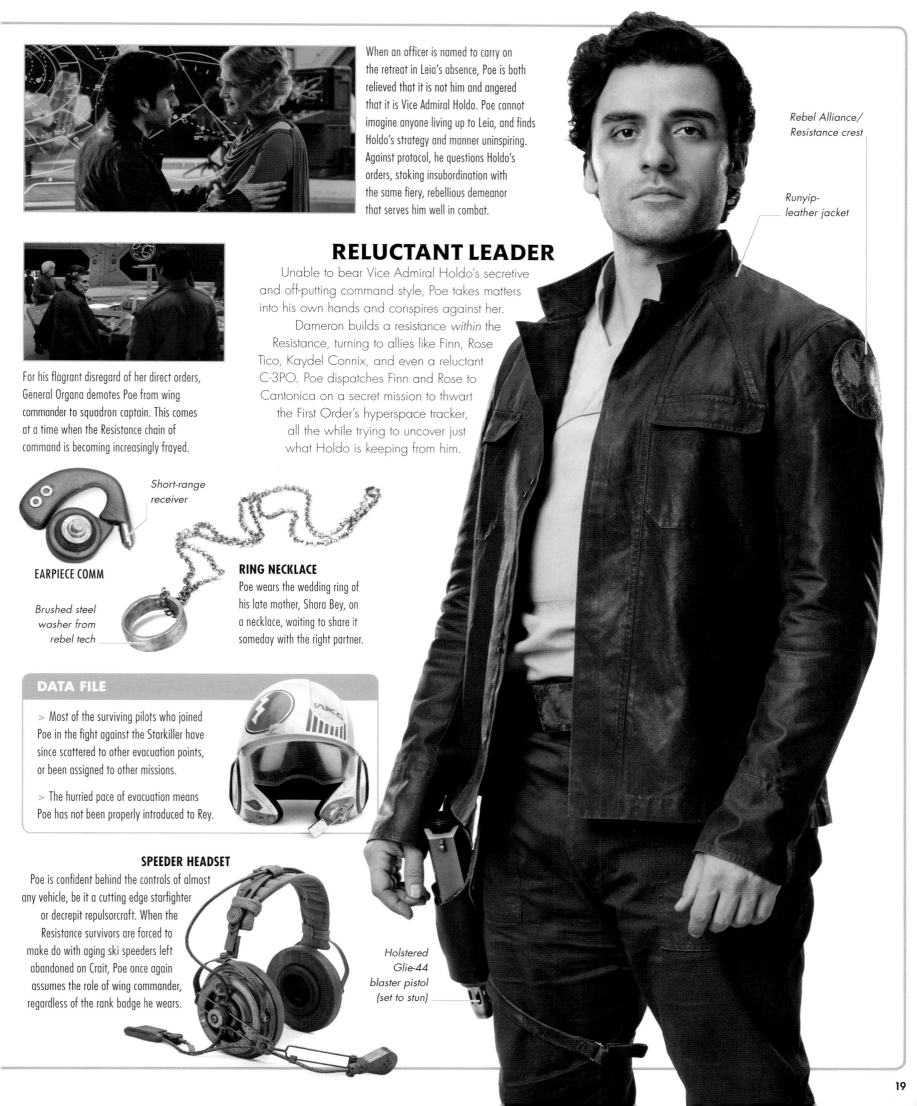

RESISTANCE DROIDS

Replaced high-frequency receiver antenna

Primary photoreceptor

Articulated holoprojector array and worklight

THE CHRONICALLY UNDERSTAFFED Resistance would not be able to operate without its extensive labor pool of droids. These tireless workers assist the flesh-and-blood personnel and keep the weapons, starships, and other machinery of the movement functioning while asking for little in return. The Resistance, proudly honoring the egalitarian ideals of the Rebel Alliance and New Republic, treats these droids not as property but as sentient beings. Rather than restricting their access to escape vessels, the Resistance allows droids equal access to them. When the decision arises, however, most droids sacrifice themselves, giving up space aboard the emergency transports for their organic crewmates.

Computer interface tool-bay disc

Bherring-24 blinkcode processing indicator

With so much happening in the span of only a few days, BB-8's processors are working overtime to keep up. A byproduct of this increased activity is an amplified spirit of adventure within the little droid.

BB-8

Though BB-8 is exhibiting greater risk-taking behavior himself, he frets over the wellbeing of his newfound friends. After extracting an astromech-to-astromech promise from R2-D2 that R2 would watch over Rey, BB-8 has kept a concerned photoreceptor on the recovering Finn. The little droid has come to trust the former stormtrooper, but recognizes that Finn needs extra guardianship.

DATA FILE

> Resistance droids often feature extended-usage power cells due to a lack of regular downtime for recharging.

> The Resistance spy droid network was ordered to lie low by C-3PO prior to the evacuation of D'Qar.

Tool-bay discs can be swapped for different functions

Surface sensor

Retractable arms

Cranial tool bay access door

Audio receiver

R4-X2

Y5-X2

Powerbus cables

Ankle articulation and power cell mount bracket

Red markings denote expanded role during crisis situations

RESISTANCE ASTROMECHS

With its emphasis on starfighters and other small space transports, the Resistance has a higher proportional need for astromechs than does its First Order enemy. Reliable R-series astromechs still see extensive use, even though some models are nearing a century of continuous operation.

Sensor and communications receiver planes

Versatile vocabulator port

Primary power coupler

In the hangar bay of the *Raddus*, the loading droid B-U4D works fast to get starfighters ready for combat.

PZ-4CO

A helpful communications droid who operated out of the command center on D'Qar, PZ-4CO is given a crucial role in the D'Qar evacuation by Lieutenant Connix. Peazy becomes an assistant evacuation coordinator, using the base and shipboard comm systems to guide Resistance groups to their emergency stations. Once aboard the *Raddus*, Peazy's next function is as a first-aid medic and duty nurse, helping monitor the health of those injured during the Resistance retreat.

RESISTANCE BB-UNITS

The Resistance's unreliable supply chain means its droid contingent is a mixture of modern units and serviceable antiques. Crew supervisors have found that occasionally pairing current-generation BB-units with decades-old R-series astromechs causes both types to learn from each other.

Security-grade photoreceptor with telescopic lens

Resistance crest on otherwise unpainted shell

Tool-bay slot filled with extended operations battery

BB-4

2BB-2

RESISTANCE BOMBERS

Armored flight deck

Rear gunner ball turret

Stabilizer foil and laser cannon mount

Sublight engine

HELPING COVER the Resistance evacuation by targeting the Dreadnought that threatens the fleet are two small squadrons of heavy bombers. The ships of Cobalt and Crimson Squadrons must withstand the devastating firepower of point-defense cannons spread across the Dreadnought's surface, then soar into bombing range to drop their massive payloads. Resistance escort starfighters fly support and interference, keeping TIE fighters away from the ponderous, explosives-laden craft. It is a costly mission—well-targeted fire from First Order gunners can erupt a bomber's entire magazine with catastrophic results. The bomber crews know the risks involved and are willing to sacrifice everything to buy their comrades a chance to escape.

MG-100 STARFORTRESS

Dating back to the final days of the Galactic Civil War, when the New Republic besieged stubborn Imperial holdouts, the Slayn & Korpil MG-100 StarFortress heavy bomber saw reduced manufacture during the decades of peace that followed. Disarmed versions of the vessel see continued use in planetary civilian services, as the modular bomb magazine can easily be repurposed for remote cargo drops, wildfire suppression, and the deployment of mining explosives. The MG-100's relatively simple and sturdy construction has ensured its longevity.

Targeting sensor mast

Ventral gunner ball turret

Bomb magazine "clip"

Plate can slide forward to form blast visor

COBALT HAMMER CREW

The *Cobalt Hammer* soars through the thick of enemy fire thanks to the bravery and tenacity of its crew. The standard assigned crew consists of bombardier Nix Jerd, pilot Finch Dallow, two specialist gunners, and a flight engineer.

NIX JERD

PAIGE TICO'S HELMET

Personalized helmet art

NIX JERD'S HELMET

PROTON BOMBS

The StarFortress's tall profile comes from the modular bombing magazine (called the "clip" by the bomber's crew). The assembly can be programmed to drop specific sections of the payload in sequence, but the most common configuration is "deploy all," which drops all 1,048 bombs from one end of the racks to the other.

Guidenhauser ejection seat flight harness

Magnetic attraction plates

Hand-scrawled messages from ordnance crew

DATA FILE

> Bombs don't technically "drop" in microgravity, but are impelled from their racks by sequenced electromagnetic plates in the clip. The bombs are then drawn magnetically to their unfortunate targets.

VENTRAL BALL TURRET

Suspended beneath the bomb racks of a StarFortress, encased in an armored transparisteel shell, is a rotating turret with a pair of heavy repeating laser cannons. Though deflector shields protect the gunner, the feeling of being exposed to enemy fire is unshakable.

Merr-Sonn Munitions EM-1919 paired repeating laser cannons

Escort duty is one of the toughest assignments for a starfighter pilot, as their ordinarily swift vessel must sacrifice its speed advantage to stay close to its assigned bomber. TIE fighters try to lure the Resistance escorts away, leaving the StarFortresses exposed.

PAIGE TICO

Paige Tico serves as the *Cobalt Hammer*'s ventral gunner. She and her sister, Rose, have committed their lives to the Resistance cause, having witnessed firsthand the brutality of the First Order on their homeworld in the Otomok system. Paige has survived several missions, and has become superstitious as a result, occasionally wrapping her medallion around the struts of her cannons for good luck. Though Rose is currently on assignment aboard the cruiser *Raddus*, she sometimes accompanies her sister on flights. In the downtime between bombing runs, Paige and Rose discuss their chance to see the galaxy.

Synthetic aviator flight cap, lined to catch perspiration

PAIGE'S MEDALLION

Buoyancy-foam filled flight vest collar

Defusing sequencer pins in sleeve stowage

Life-support system atmosphere hose

Control button

BOMB RELEASE

The bombardier sights a target from a pedestal on the flight deck that contains a concentrated sensor feed. The system calculates the optimum time for release, and at a given prompt, or at the discretion of the bombardier, the control button on a wireless remote triggers the release of the payload.

RESISTANCE STARFIGHTERS

THE FIGHT AGAINST the Starkiller nearly exhausted the supply of starfighters stationed on D'Qar, but thankfully that was not the extent of the Resistance's resources. Distress calls sent during that crisis have drawn reinforcements in the form of the starfighter complements of the newly arrived cruisers. This not only brings in X-wings to replenish Blue and Red Squadrons, but also adds the blazingly fast A-wings to General Organa and Admiral Ackbar's roster. These fighters are primarily tasked with covering the retreat of the beleaguered Resistance fleet.

As fighters are redistributed among the Resistance squadrons, they fall under Poe Dameron's command, and the hangar bays of the *Raddus* become their primary launch point.

Synthsilk scarf, a gift from her father

FreiTek life-support unit

"DA" stands for "Deadly Approach," the punchline to a well-known pilots' joke

Towing slot for assisted moving of landed craft

Guidenhauser ejection harness

TALLISSAN "TALLIE" LINTRA

At 22 years of age, Lieutenant Tallissan Lintra was born long after the dark days of the Galactic Empire. She has proven to be one of the most capable pilots in the Resistance, dazzling even the hard-to-impress Poe Dameron with her skills. Tallie learned the basics of piloting behind the controls of an old RZ-1 A-wing that her father used as a cropduster on their farm on Pippip 3.

RONITH BLARIO

Swiveling cannon mounting

Novaldex K-88 Event Horizon engines

Missile launcher

RZ-2 A-WING INTERCEPTOR

Already decades old, the RZ-2 is nonetheless an upgrade of the venerable RZ-1 A-wing starfighter that played a crucial role in the Galactic Civil War. Improvements include refined cannon mountings, a streamlined hull, and more powerful jammers that make the A-wing a less tempting target for enemy sensors. Tallie flies an A-wing with blue livery.

T-70 X-WING

With the New Republic's T-85 X-wing fleet atomized by the destruction of the Hosnian system, the Resistance's T-70s are once again the most advanced examples of this legendary design.

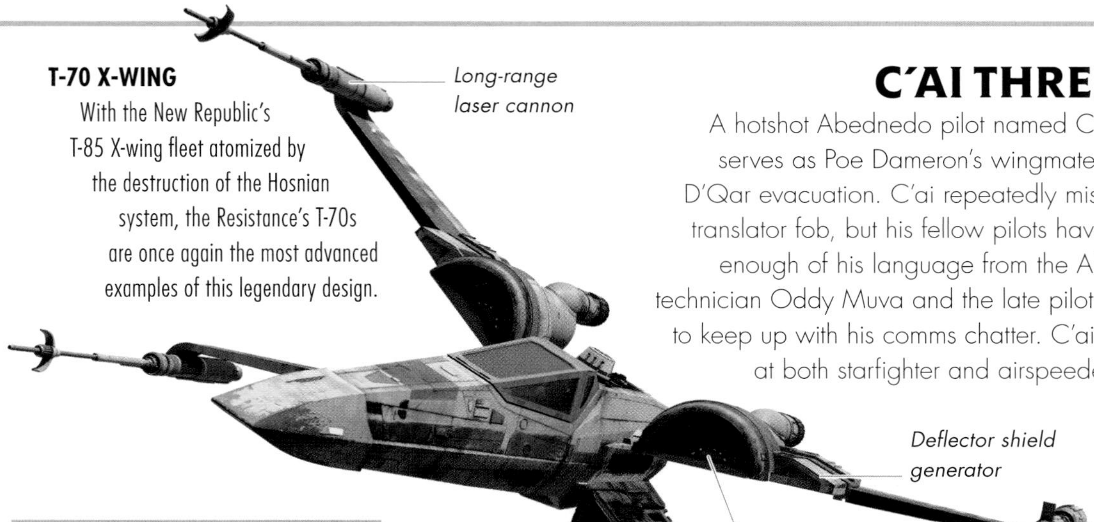

Long-range laser cannon
Deflector shield generator
Electromagnetic gyroscope

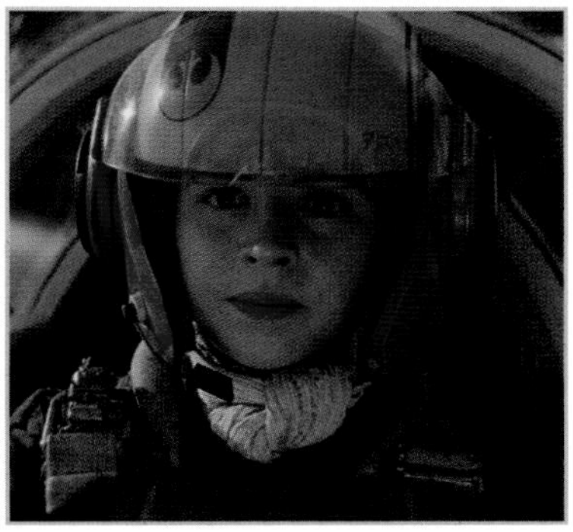

Resistance starfighter squadrons are far more improvised than those of more formal military forces. Squadron names are simple and recyclable—a pilot who flew in Blue Squadron for one engagement may form part of Red Squadron in another.

C'AI THRENALLI

A hotshot Abednedo pilot named C'ai Threnalli serves as Poe Dameron's wingmate during the D'Qar evacuation. C'ai repeatedly misplaces his translator fob, but his fellow pilots have learned enough of his language from the Abednedo technician Oddy Muva and the late pilot Ello Asty to keep up with his comms chatter. C'ai is skilled at both starfighter and airspeeder piloting.

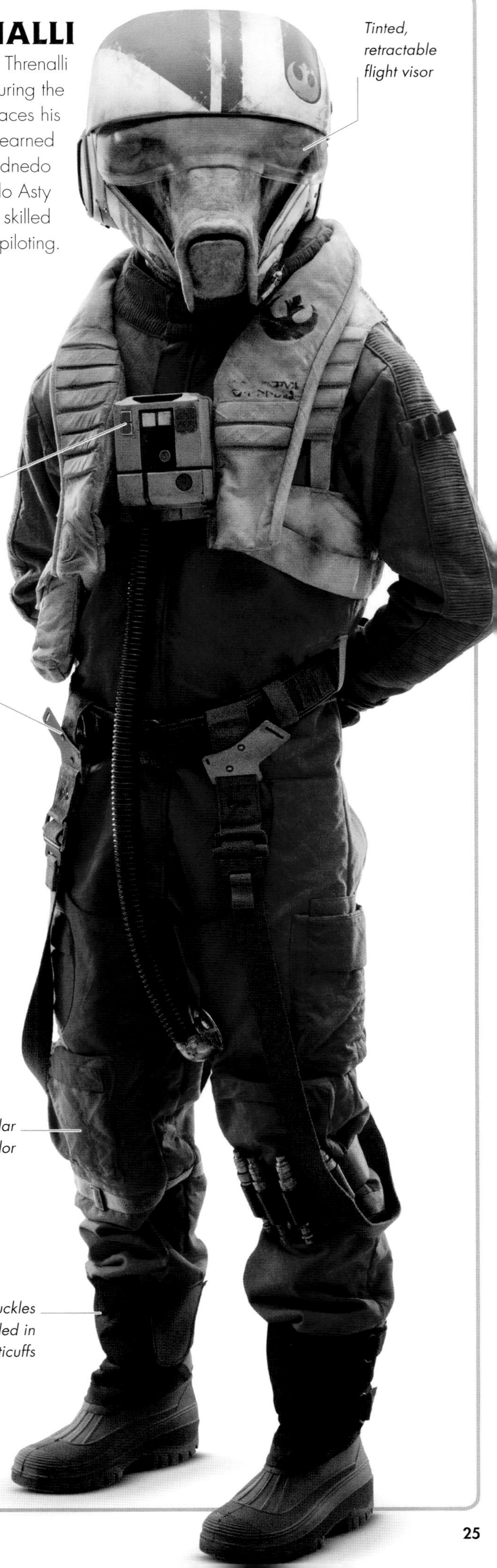

Tinted, retractable flight visor
Life-support activation switch
Reinforced gear terrets
"Interstellar orange" color
Vibro-knuckles concealed in boot for fisticuffs

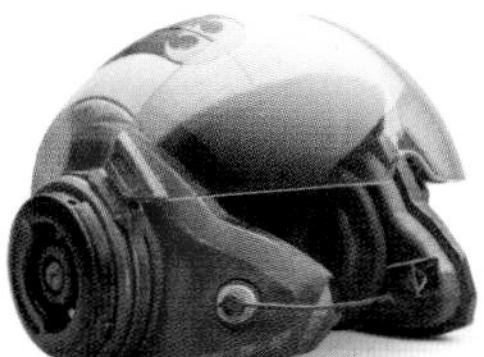

TALLIE'S HELMET

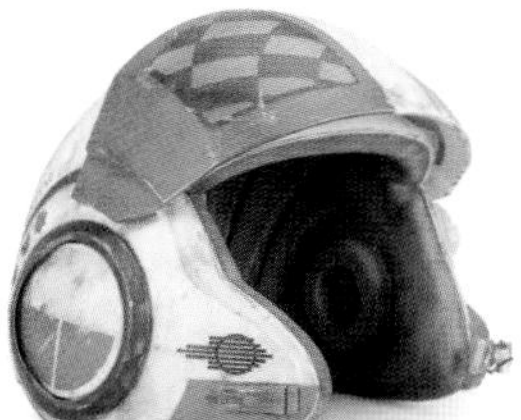

STARCK'S HELMET

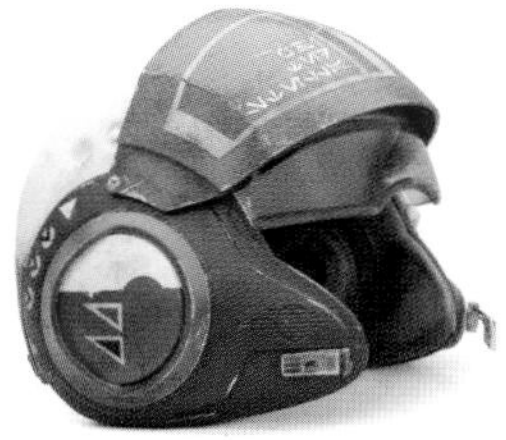

TUBBS' HELMET

Signal flares

STOMERONI STARCK

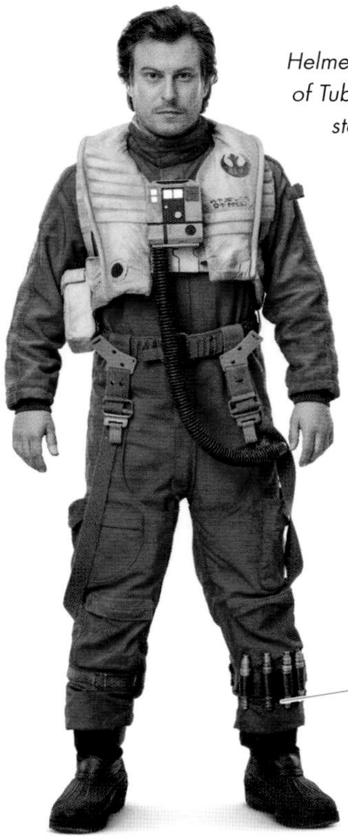

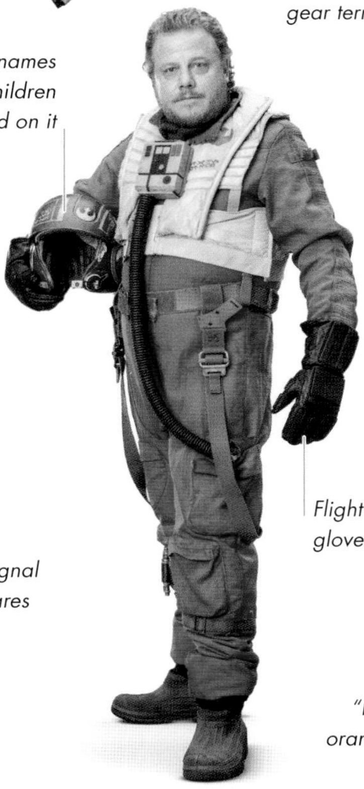

Helmet has names of Tubbs' children stenciled on it
Flight gloves

JAYCRIS TUBBS

DATA FILE

> As was the case with the Rebellion, the Resistance has more pilots than it does craft. Pilots are often on standby, awaiting deployment.

> During the Resistance exodus from D'Qar, many fighter aces serve as lifeboat and transport pilots instead.

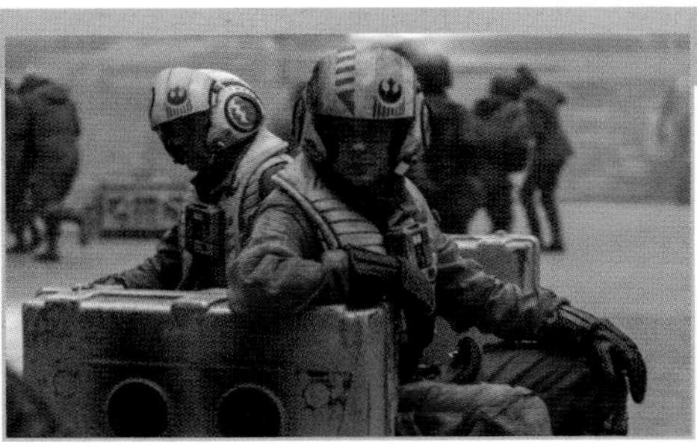

GENERAL HUX

ARMITAGE HUX is basking in his own glory. Under his command, the Starkiller weapon proved successful, despite its subsequent destruction. His vision of superior technology, precise conquest, and the methodical deployment of forces has decimated the New Republic. The next technological terror in Hux's arsenal is ready to be deployed—active hyperspace tracking. Originally explored in its infancy by the secret Imperial think tank known as the Tarkin Initiative, it has now evolved from theory into reality. Hux's engineers have perfected the system, creating a devastating countermeasure that tracks Resistance ships through hyperspace, making escape impossible.

Remorseless gaze

Gaberwool expedition greatcoat

Hux loathes Kylo Ren, and takes pleasure both in Kylo's failures and Snoke's anger with his apprentice. The fact that Kylo had to be rescued from Starkiller Base after being bested by a lightsaber novice delights the young general.

DESTROYER OF WORLDS

Hux is responsible for the deaths of billions, having given the order to fire the Starkiller at the heavily populated Hosnian system. A man of no scruples who craves power above all, Hux has dispatched many enemies or would-be foes before they became too dangerous a threat. This included quietly eliminating his own father, the elder General Brendol Hux, whose elevated position in the early First Order gave Armitage a childhood of great privilege.

Hux hides a monomolecular-blade dagger in his sleeve

Basic sight also serves as mount for custom scopes

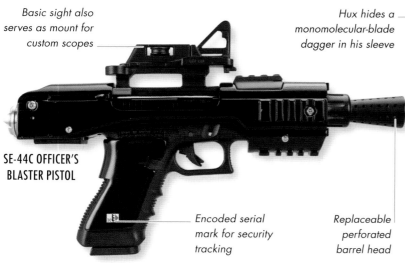

SE-44C OFFICER'S BLASTER PISTOL

Encoded serial mark for security tracking

Replaceable perforated barrel head

The *Finalizer* is Hux's dedicated flagship, but when it flies in formation with Snoke's *Supremacy*, Hux often transfers to the larger vessel, leaving Captain Peavey in command. Hux covets the *Supremacy*, but tries to hide such thoughts, aware that they may betray him to Kylo Ren and Supreme Leader Snoke.

Volume control

CONTROLLER'S INTERCOM HEADSET

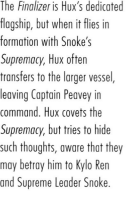

Crested command cap with insignia

Fake code cylinder contains poison

Rank cylinder encoded with Hux's command clearance

First Order insignia

Unit is mounted on bridge bulkhead

Tough plastoid shell

Primary holo-camera

Holoprojector lens

HOLOPROJECTOR

Supreme Leader Snoke has eyes throughout the First Order fleet. Though he rarely ventures from the confines of his flagship, he can observe events and transmit his image through dedicated holoprojectors.

Traditional flared-hip breeches

DATA FILE

> Hux's direct access to Snoke effectively gives him a rank higher than general, but Snoke refuses to grant Hux his desired title of "grand marshal."

> Hux's delicate ego is stung when Poe Dameron deliberately mispronounces his name as "General Hugs."

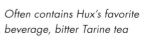

Often contains Hux's favorite beverage, bitter Tarine tea

PETTY OFFICER LANK PAZE

HUX'S STAFF

As Hux transfers his command between various ships and facilities, a team of hand-picked officers keeps his affairs in order while accompanying him. The stern Captain Tritt Opan has worked with Hux for years, and was a junior aide under Brendol Hux before him. Opan is skilled at carrying out Hux's dirty work, from assassination to sabotage, in order to ensure that no enemy—whether First Order or otherwise—can get the better of the general. Opan is tight-lipped about such duties, for he knows Hux could just as easily have him eliminated, if he so wished.

OFFICER'S INSULATED DRINKING CUP

CAPTAIN TRITT OPAN

KYLO REN

HAVING BEEN THWARTED by Rey on Starkiller Base, Kylo Ren has to answer to his unforgiving mentor, the cruel Supreme Leader Snoke. The heinous act of killing Han Solo has driven Kylo deeper into the grip of the dark side, at great personal pain—he is now more conflicted and torn than ever, further destabilizing an already dangerous man. He obediently carries out the Supreme Leader's orders to pursue and cripple the fleeing Resistance, but Snoke's berating punishments weigh on him, opening hidden emotional wounds just as his physical ones are healing.

Delicate multiceps for injury treatment

MEDICAL DROID
An IT-S00.2 medical droid tends to the lightsaber slashes Kylo suffered across his chest and face, and the bowcaster wound to his abdomen. Although they are sealed with mechnosutures, bacta therapy is applied too late to prevent scarring.

Kylo's dogged pursuit of the Resistance leads him to the abandoned world of Crait, where at last his hunger to deliver vengeance by lightsaber blade may be sated.

Partially exposed inner workings allow for easy modifications and upkeep

Static-damping fabric in cape grounds electrical interference

THIRST FOR POWER
Kylo has sacrificed everything in his commitment to the dark side, rejecting his family through his pledge of loyalty to Supreme Leader Snoke. But Han Solo's warning that Snoke is only using Kylo for his power echoes through Kylo's mind. Now that the First Order campaign to retake the galaxy is truly underway, Kylo plots his future through uncertain times. With ambition fueled by the dark side, Kylo prioritizes his own survival and ultimate ascension.

KYLO REN'S LIGHTSABER

DATA FILE

> From the bridge of his command shuttle, Kylo leads the First Order siege of Crait, an engagement he hopes will spell the end of the hated Resistance. However, Kylo lets his emotions, the source of his power, cloud his tactical reasoning.

Ragged lightsaber
blade leaves trail
of embers with
each swing

Shaft contains
bifurcated
kyber crystal

DARK DESTINY

Kylo has long been under the dark influence of Snoke, who has fanned the embers of resentment and isolation in Ben Solo into a white-hot anger. While Kylo projects the air of an obedient servant, he cleverly plots his own path to regain the status and power he has lost to Rey's blade. The fate of the mysterious scavenger from Jakku is inextricably connected to his, and Kylo cannot deny the bond they share in the Force.

Helmet smashed into
shards in a fit of rage

SHATTERED HELMET

KYLO'S CHAMBERS

Rescued from the Starkiller disaster, Kylo returns to his quarters aboard the *Supremacy*, Supreme Leader Snoke's vast flagship. Here, Kylo's isolation allows him to meditate on the Force. He has left Darth Vader's charred helmet aboard the *Finalizer*, perhaps not ready to face that visage until he recovers from his failure.

Heavy laser
cannon

Shielded and
armored cockpit

Transport
Corps flight
helmet

Densely-layered solar
collector surfaces

TIE SILENCER

STARFIGHTER ASSAULT

Kylo has inherited the amazing piloting skills of his father and grandfather, bolstered by his Force abilities. In pursuit of the Resistance fleet, Kylo boards his prototype TIE silencer, leading Special Forces starfighters to penetrate the fleeing ships' defenses. Kylo fires a volley of torpedoes that destroys the *Raddus'* hangar bay, but finds he cannot open fire on the warship's vulnerable bridge—a decision that is ultimately taken from him by a less conflicted wingmate.

Retractable ordnance
bay in wing joint

**LIEUTENANT JOBER TAVSON,
KYLO'S SHUTTLE PILOT**

FIRST ORDER FLEET

THE DISCOVERY of the Resistance base's location leads to the dramatic arrival of the First Order fleet at D'Qar. Spearheading the assault is the *Finalizer*, the *Resurgent*-class Star Destroyer under General Hux's direct command. Even this overwhelming force is merely the first wave of a larger offensive. The true scale of the First Order military is beyond even General Organa's worst-case projections. In the shadowy corners of uncharted space—and within the hidden ledgers of scheming weapons manufacturers—the First Order has been secretly building for war. With the New Republic fleet vaporized by the Starkiller, it now stands unopposed.

Despite their impressive firepower, the First Order's capital ships fail to inflict critical damage on the *Raddus*. Instead, it is a squadron of tiny starfighters that lands the most devastating blow.

Worry lines publicly display private doubts

Officer rank cylinders

Point-defense turrets cover upper surface

Command bridge

THE *FULMINATRIX*

The duty of laying waste to D'Qar falls to the *Fulminatrix*, a *Mandator IV*-class Siege Dreadnought. The lower surface of this enormous craft hangs heavy with orbital-bombardment cannons, which can punch through planetary shields and tear apart capital ships. Smaller cannons along its topside defend the *Fulminatrix* from starfighter attack while it rains destruction from the skies.

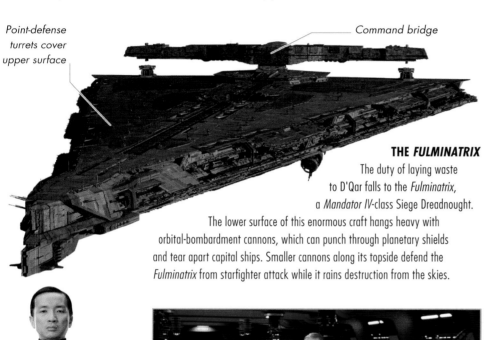

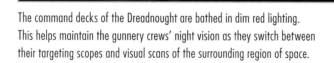

The command decks of the Dreadnought are bathed in dim red lighting. This helps maintain the gunnery crews' night vision as they switch between their targeting scopes and visual scans of the surrounding region of space.

CAPTAIN CANADY

The commander of the *Fulminatrix*, Captain Moden Canady, served aboard the Star Destroyer *Solicitude* during the time of the Galactic Empire. Now in his 50s, he is surrounded by First Order personnel half his age and is dismayed by their youth. While he can appreciate and empathize with their zeal, their untested nature and failure to work effectively as a team chafes against his operational discipline. He is proud of his starship's power, but wishes it had a crew worthy of its destructive potential.

WARRANT OFFICER SUDAY BASCUS

TIE PILOT CORPS

The TIE fighter pilots of the First Order are particularly driven to destroy the Resistance. It was the failure of the Starkiller's TIE defenses that led to its loss, and now the surviving pilots are eager to prove their worth.

Ship-linked targeting sensors

Life-support unit

Lieutenant Poldin LeHuse, formerly part of the Starkiller aerial defense force, is newly reassigned to Kylo Ren's personal squadron. He holds nothing back in his desire to make the Resistance suffer.

LIEUTENANT POLDIN LEHUSE

Faceted armored viewport

Solar collector array

TIE/FO STARFIGHTER

TIE/SF STARFIGHTER

Heavy weapons turret

First Order symbol

DATA FILE

> First Order crews develop intense loyalty to their starships, spending most of their time aboard a single vessel.

> The Resistance counts at least 30 Star Destroyers engaged in the pursuit of its fleet.

Primary command bridge

THE *FINALIZER*

The *Finalizer* continues to serve as General Hux's command ship, leading the siege of D'Qar and coordinating the initial pursuit of the Resistance. With the arrival of Supreme Leader Snoke's enormous flagship, the *Finalizer* moves to a support role.

Heavy turbolaser batteries

Pursuit and combat command bridge

Much like the Empire, First Order design accentuates the idea of command hierarchies, with bridge officers literally afforded a higher platform than the noncommissioned crew working in sunken pits.

Upper deck superstructure

CAPTAIN PEAVEY

Another Imperial veteran, Edrison Peavey is older than his commanding officer, Armitage Hux, and was a contemporary of Armitage's father, the late General Brendol Hux. Watching the younger Hux advance through scheming and nepotism has soured Peavey's view of the man, but he is professional enough an officer to keep his deep disrespect silent.

THE *SUPREMACY*

EMERGING FROM HYPERSPACE to eclipse the First Order fleet is the flagship of Supreme Leader Snoke, the *Supremacy*. The only *Mega*-class Star Destroyer in existence, the *Supremacy* is the command headquarters of the fleet. It is a giant wing, 60 kilometers wide, which blurs the line between capital ship and mobile space station. The *Supremacy*'s interior not only carries entire armies into battle, but also serves as an industrial complex on a vast scale. Its enormous shipyards and manufacturing facilities can assemble and repair vehicles ranging in size from scout walkers to Star Destroyers.

SNOKE'S HEADQUARTERS

Snoke has no throne world, and has not rooted the First Order to a single planet that serves as its capital. Instead, he prefers to rule from within the safety of the *Supremacy*, staying ever mobile and maneuvering First Order agents onto countless worlds. Though Starkiller Base represented a sizable concentration of First Order power, Snoke's preparations meant that its destruction did not set back the regime's invasion plans.

COMMAND BRIDGE
The primary command bridge is found within the tower that caps the huge terraced structure at the center of the ship. From here, wraparound viewports provide a sweeping vista of the city-like structures that line the wing.

Shielded bridge tower

Throne room

Engines line rear edge of wing

Forward artillery escarpment and docking bay band

Habitable "city" sprawl

Targeting data is projected onto visor

FLEET GUNNERS

Lining the *Supremacy*'s surface are artillery emplacements that can lob devastating plasma volleys at any target foolish enough to come too close. First Order gunners fire at the retreating Resistance fleet, keeping up a steady barrage that pummels any fleeing ships that stray within cannon range.

Multi-spectrum photoreceptor with telescoping lens

FIRST ORDER DROIDS

Unlike the Resistance, which values the individuality of droids, the First Order treats its machines as machines, resulting in cold personalities. Even the normally friendly BB-unit model has taken a sinister turn. BB-9E, for example, seems downright malicious when reporting transgressions.

Grilled openings permit ventilation and enhanced sensor transparency

BB-9E

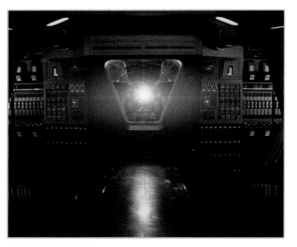

TRACKING ROOM

At the heart of the *Supremacy*'s advanced hyperspace tracker is a complex static hyperspace field generator. This envelops arrays of databanks and computers in a localized hyperspace field that accelerates their calculation speeds to unimaginable rates.

GUNNER BRUN OBATSUN

> Snoke concealed the *Supremacy* in the Unknown Regions, masking its immense sensor signature by hiding it in close proximity to highly energetic stars.

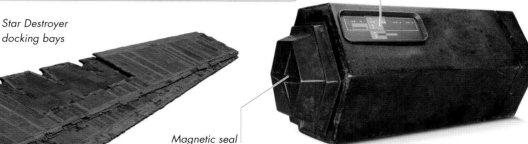

The communications complex monitors the galaxy's holonet traffic, identifying trends and weaknesses the First Order can exploit. Orders are dispatched to agents operating in New Republic and independent space.

Star Destroyer docking bays

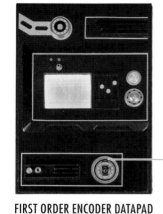

Indicators show crate contains foodstuffs

Magnetic seal keeps contents fresh

SUPPLY CRATE

LIEUTENANT LUSICA STYNNIX

Code cylinder port

FIRST ORDER ENCODER DATAPAD

WAR MACHINE

The *Supremacy*'s crew numbers in the millions, all carrying out Supreme Leader Snoke's escalating plan of conquest. On the operations decks, floors of open workstations bustle with efficient controllers. Many of the crew are subadults—too young for active combat deployment—and are among the First Order's most loyal servants. These personnel have been fully indoctrinated into First Order mythology—the idea of a chaotic galaxy requiring strong, unflinching order to bring it under control.

Work gloves have electro-sensitive fingertips that permit touch-screen access

Operations division status datapad

Rank sash commemorating Imperial Admiral Clyss Power

JUNIOR OFFICERS

Whereas Imperial youth brigades were largely symbolic pledges of patriotism, the First Order puts its youth into actual military service. Raised since birth in the First Order fold, these subadults have a natural competitive streak that drives them to excel.

GUNNERY CHIEF PEERA MASO

SCAN-OPS PETTY OFFICER RUMITAR SHAY

SUPREME LEADER SNOKE

THOUGH HIS NAME is known to the galaxy and his reputation as the Supreme Leader of the First Order precedes him, few have ever seen Snoke in the flesh. He obscures himself with distance, being forever unreachable save for a select few who can contact him directly. Even under such circumstances, Snoke disguises his true nature. Whatever frailties have broken his body are dwarfed by the immense size at which he typically projects his form.

HEART OF DARKNESS

Snoke is powerful in the dark side of the Force, but he is no Sith. That thousand-year lineage stretching from Darth Bane to the last Sith Lord, Darth Vader, was undone when Vader died destroying his mentor, Darth Sidious. The fulfillment of an ancient prophecy foretold the end of the Sith, but it never predicted the end of darkness.

Hypertrophic scar channel

Corded auropyle fabric khalat robes

Misshapen face from malformed zygoma

Snoke's painful stance has caused him to prioritize comfort

Obsidian from catacombs beneath Darth Vader's Mustafar castle

Enlarged brains can process multidimensional calculations

SLIPPERS

Gold etched with glyphs of the Dwartii

RING

Amplification lenses assist naturally weak eyes

THRONE ROOM

Snoke's throne room aboard the _Supremacy_ is an enormous chamber veiled by an opaque red curtain. It is from here that Snoke broadcasts his image, magnified into a towering giant, across the First Order's territories.

Dark purple robes, meant to evoke the royal hues of old Imperial advisors

ATTENDANTS

Snoke's retinue includes mute alien navigators who originated in the Unknown Regions. Were it not for the ancient hyperspace trails blazed by these towering servants, the Imperial survivors who fled into this uncharted realm would certainly have perished. These navigators designed and operate the oculus viewing scope in Snoke's throne room.

Robes conceal segmented, chitinous plates

PRAETORIAN GUARD

Eight Praetorians flank Snoke's throne, their red armor blending into the curtain that surrounds the chamber. They stand as implacable, unmoving sentinels, but should any hostility surface from Snoke's rare invited guests, they snap instantly into combat stances.

E

Ben Solo as his apprentice as
ly someone of the Skywalker
d destroy the last Jedi.

ysical skills may have faded,
aided abilities to persuade,
and perceive are tremendous.

PRAETORIAN GUARD

THE PRAETORIAN GUARD are a bold example of an Imperial symbol reimagined, distorted, and aggrandized by the First Order. These elite sentinels stand watch over Supreme Leader Snoke's throne room aboard his flagship. Their brilliant red uniforms are a deliberate echo of those worn by Emperor Palpatine's Royal Guard, but the pageantry of the robes has been swept aside to allow an unhindered view of precision-machined combat armor. The Praetorians are the ultimate close-circle guard, eschewing ranged weaponry. They are the last line of defense protecting Snoke, ready to destroy any threat that would dare penetrate so deeply into the First Order's heart.

WARRIORS OF SNOKE

Supreme Leader Snoke's first line of defense is his reclusiveness. His reputation looms large over First Order territories, but he rarely makes public appearances, preferring instead to transmit his image across light years as a hologram. Very few ever see him in the flesh, and those that are afforded an audience with the Supreme Leader are kept within lethal distance of his ever-vigilant Praetorians. Snoke's Force abilities are strong, but his body is broken, his stride staggered, and his muscles weak. He relies instead on the combat prowess of his crimson protectors.

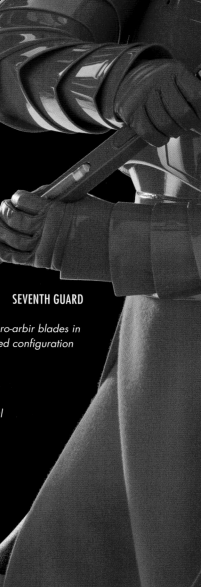

Flared composite armor helmet with mag-field conductors

SEVENTH GUARD

Twin vibro-arbir blades in connected configuration

Scintillating electro-plasma blade

Ultrasonic vibrational blade cradle

Eight soldiers make up the Praetorian Guard. With their all-enveloping uniforms, their identities are completely concealed. The First Order aesthetic heavily favors symmetry ("What is past is future"), so they are actually four sets of pairs, with each pair brandishing the same weapons.

Tempered micro-edge carbonite blade

Electro-chain whip

Electro-bisento tempered blade surface

Large pauldrons to deflect vertical strikes

Segmented plate armor allows for flexibility

Greaves protect lower legs

ARMORED GUARDIANS

The layered armor of the Praetorian Guard is a high-tech onion-skin of laminate, impregnated with conductive wirepaths that, once powered, create an intense local magnetic field. Once this energy-intensive field activates, the powered plates can deflect blaster fire. Even a lightsaber will glance off, though a directed thrust will penetrate the shell. The mag-coils are costly, the plates heavy, and mag-field exposure is ultimately painful to the wearer, but such are the sacrifices of protecting the Supreme Leader. The Praetorians endure this out of unswerving loyalty and duty.

THIRD GUARD

FIRST GUARD

PRAETORIAN WEAPONS

The Praetorians carry weapons that are high-tech versions of unpowered analogues found in primitive societies across the galaxy. Each tempered metal blade is connected to a compact ultrasonic generator that creates a high-frequency vibration across the cutting edge, increasing its lethality. Parallel to each cutting edge is an electro-plasma filament that creates an energized blade capable of parrying a lightsaber.

BILARI ELECTRO-CHAIN WHIP (ARTICULATED CONFIGURATION)

Electro-plasma filament

TWIN VIBRO-ARBIR BLADES (SEPARATED)

VIBRO-VOULGE

Power cell in hilt

Ultrasonic generator

ELECTRO-BISENTO

ROSE TICO

A HARDWORKING member of the Resistance support crew, Rose Tico has hated the First Order since she was a child. Rose grew up on the impoverished mining colony of Hays Minor, the smaller world in a double-planet configuration in the Otomok system. These worlds were far beyond the scope of the New Republic's policing efforts, and unknown to the galaxy at large, the system fell under the sway of the expanding First Order. In secret, the First Order tested its weapons on the populace and stole children to turn into stormtroopers. Rose is now finally able to fight back against her sworn enemy.

Dark hair common on Otomok worlds

Duty uniform identification plaque

Self-coded override data spikes

Adjustable utility belt with cargo loops

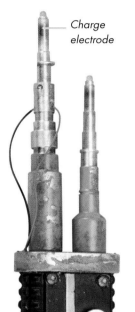

Charge electrode

Intensity dial below trigger button

ELECTRO-SHOCK PROD

Rose spends most of her time deep in the inner workings of starships, her mastery of technology essential to keeping the rickety vessels of the Resistance operational. She is the first to admit that her people skills need work.

FLIGHT TECHNICIAN

Rose is an imaginative mechanic. Her innovations include a baffle system that makes the Resistance's bombers harder to detect by enemy sensors. This modification is also being rolled out into Resistance escape craft—an unusual modification for such vessels, which ordinarily use powerful automatic distress beacons to alert anyone in the vicinity of a ship in crisis. The Resistance, however, desperately needs to keep a low profile, even if that means hiding emergency craft from potential aid.

ROSE'S MEDALLION

Rose's medallion is a stylized ensign of the Otomok system, representing Hays Minor. It is made of pure Haysian smelt, a transition metal with incredibly efficient conductive properties. It is the partner medallion of the one worn by Paige Tico.

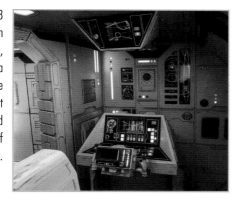

Rose, Finn, and BB-8 leave the fleet on an unsanctioned mission, sneaking off in a transport pod. The vessel is the smallest hyperspace-enabled ship capable of reaching Cantonica.

TRANSPORT POD

Rose's shuttle is the modified control pod of a Resistance transport, which began life as a B-wing Mark II cockpit. Its small size and Rose's skill at keeping engine flux below sensor thresholds mean that Rose and Finn can depart the fleet without being detected. Though Rose doesn't consider herself a great pilot, she has much more experience behind the controls than Finn.

Stabilizer fin

Durasteel armored cockpit

Docking hatch

Canto Bight's opulence provokes very different reactions in Rose and Finn. While Finn is seduced by the resort's grandeur, Rose sees its guests for the war profiteers and criminals that they really are.

RESISTANCE FIGHTER

Rose gives her all during the struggle against the First Order, repeatedly risking her life for the cause. Her parents, Hue and Thanya, raised her with a strong sense of right and wrong, and her sister, five years her elder, also provided guidance. In more peaceful times, Rose and Paige would daydream about traveling the galaxy, but the evil of the First Order has now made that impossible. Though intensely focused, Rose must try not to let her temper get the better of her.

Wear and tear of adventure

Salt dust from Crait

Resistance all-weather poncho

Alliance crest is usually concealed

RESISTANCE RING

An antique from the Galactic Civil War, Rose's innocuous ring hides an Alliance crest. It was once used to show support for the Rebellion in the corridors of the Imperial Senate.

Pilfered First Order officer boots

VICE ADMIRAL HOLDO

Frequently dyed hair colored with chromomites

Defender-5 sporting blaster features stun and lethal settings

THE FIRST ORDER BLITZ against the *Raddus* decimates the Resistance leadership, requiring a dramatic shake-up in command structure. Vice Admiral Amilyn Holdo, the highest-ranking officer still able to command, transfers from the *Ninka* to take the reins of the remnant fleet. Her words of confidence are met with skepticism, however, by a crew who are mostly strangers to her command. There should be little doubt of her commitment— Holdo was part of the Rebellion from the very start of the Galactic Civil War. She has known Leia Organa since their teenage years, when both served as part of the Apprentice Legislature in the Imperial Senate. Nonetheless, some silently feel Holdo has a lot to prove.

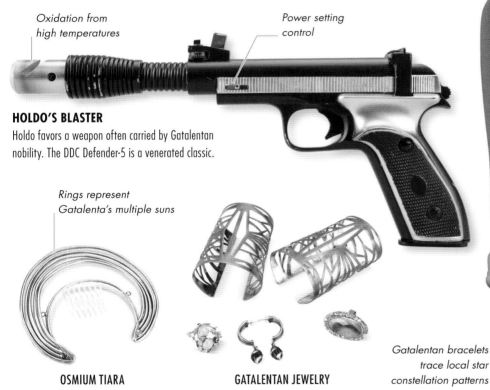

Oxidation from high temperatures

Power setting control

HOLDO'S BLASTER
Holdo favors a weapon often carried by Gatalentan nobility. The DDC Defender-5 is a venerated classic.

Rings represent Gatalenta's multiple suns

OSMIUM TIARA

GATALENTAN JEWELRY

Gatalentan bracelets trace local star constellation patterns

From the emergency bridge of the damaged *Raddus*, Amilyn Holdo announces her assumption of command in a transmission to the entire fleet. Now that it has become evident the First Order can track Resistance ships through hyperspace, options for escape dwindle as fast as the Resistance's fuel reserves.

A STRIKING APPEARANCE
Holdo doesn't wear the combat khakis and camouflage kit most often spotted in Resistance bases. Instead, her dyed hair and eye-catching clothing show her fierce devotion to her homeworld of Gatalenta and its independent spirit. Gatalenta is known across the galaxy for its poetry and the tranquility and compassion of its inhabitants.

> The *Raddus* has two command bridges—the principal dorsal one and an emergency ventral one. It is from the latter that Holdo commands.

> Holdo keeps most of her command staff aboard the *Ninka*, until depleting fuel reserves force her to evacuate its crew to the *Raddus*.

Vice Admiral Holdo has a loyal command staff of handpicked officers. The influx of these strangers adds to the already tense atmosphere aboard the Resistance flagship.

Officer's rank plaque

Tunic pocket

Integrated belt

Holstered ERD Glie-44D pistol

MAJOR NOSSIT CICER

CAPTAIN GENO NAMIT

SERGEANT DERHAM BOYCE

Resistance combat helmet (visor removed)

Weatherproof field jacket

RM-45 ammunition and tool pouch

BlasTech EL-16 blaster rifle

BRIDGE GUARDS

With the Resistance chased out of its base, all personnel are now trapped in spacebound vessels. Faced with this claustrophobic situation, ground troops have been redeployed as extra shipboard security. Tensions continue to rise as events turn increasingly dire, and these guards stand vigilant should there be any breakdown of order.

COMMANDER D'ACY

Larma D'Acy comes from a career military family entrusted with the protection of sovereign space in the Warlentta system. The demilitarization of the New Republic had little effect on her home, though her father was one of the loudest to question such a shortsighted decision. When an opportunity for her to join the Resistance arose, D'Acy's family gave their blessing for the greater good.

When Warlentta refused to join the New Republic, its independent culture made an impression on then-Senator Leia Organa. After founding the Resistance, Leia visited the world and personally recruited D'Acy.

TEMPLE ISLAND

WHEN IMPERIAL FORCES surrendered in the aftermath of the Battle of Jakku, Luke Skywalker began a lengthy quest to recover as much lost Jedi knowledge as possible. Over the years, he uncovered tantalizing clues as to the origin point of the Jedi, but its exact location remained a mystery. When he finally did piece together its location with the help of the old scholar Lor San Tekka, Skywalker kept this information to himself. An unnamed island, located in the northern latitudes of Ahch-To, was the site of the first Jedi temple. It was this world, and its temple island, where Luke would eventually hide away from the galaxy.

The suns of Ahch-To mark another dawn on a world where little ever changes. Ahch-To stands apart from the rest of the galaxy, a peaceful oasis where the daily struggles and triumphs of life are greatly removed from the ravages of interstellar war. But in many ways, the island is a microcosm of the galaxy that surrounds it.

Extra membrane enables sharp underwater vision

Traditional white habit

THALA-SIRENS

Thala-sirens are large, flippered marine mammals often found sunning themselves along the coastal rocks of the island. The docile creatures are not hunted, and thus do not fear the natives of the island, but they do produce a nutritious green milk that Luke has taken to harvesting.

Forward-facing eyes provide stereoscopic vision

NATIVE LIFE

Animal life on Ahch-To has evolved to thrive in or near the ocean. Avian forms are dominated by seabirds, and the native sentient beings of the planet have evolved from this branch of life-form. Salt glands are a common evolutionary trait, as creatures on Ahch-To are able to extract the sea salt from their food and drink. Skin, hair, and plumage also have an innate water-shedding ability afforded by natural oils.

Webbed feet assist in swimming

Feet show avian origins of species

PORGS

Porgs are a hyper-curious species of avian found throughout the islands of Ahch-To. These cliff-dwelling creatures perform controlled dives into the sea, fetching small fish to feed upon or pass to their otherwise helpless porglets.

LANAIS

The sentient Lanais are distant relatives of the porgs. An enclave of females known as the Caretakers lives on the temple island, devoted to the upkeep and care of the ancient structures that dot the landmass. The males spend most of their lives at sea.

JEDI TEMPLE
Built atop a high ledge overlooking the ocean, the temple houses meditation plinths and an ancient mosaic depicting the first Jedi.

TREE LIBRARY
The hollowed-out trunk of a centuries-old uneti tree contains a reading chamber and a bookshelf that holds sacred Jedi texts.

CARETAKER VILLAGE
The female Caretakers live in a hillside village overlooking a cove where male Lanais, or "Visitors," make regular landings.

MIRROR CAVE
A natural convergence of energy, strong in the dark side of the Force, manifests itself on the eastern side of the island.

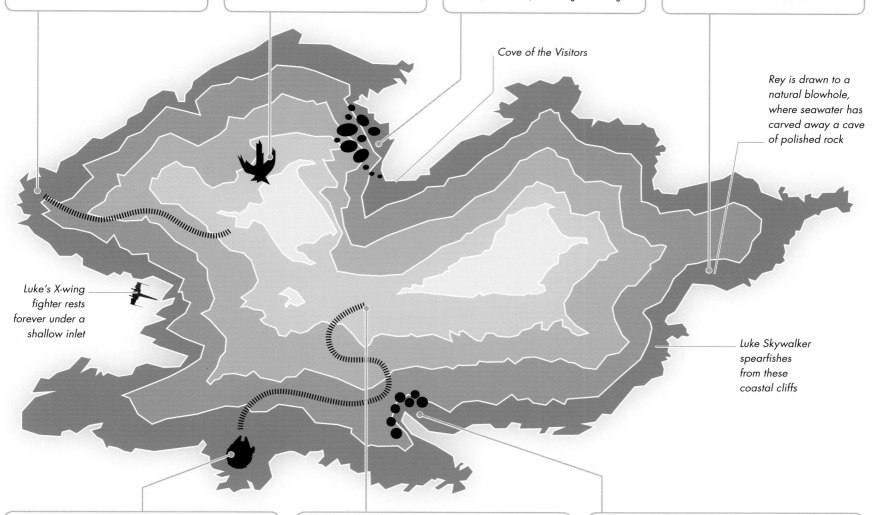

Cove of the Visitors

Rey is drawn to a natural blowhole, where seawater has carved away a cave of polished rock

Luke's X-wing fighter rests forever under a shallow inlet

Luke Skywalker spearfishes from these coastal cliffs

MILLENNIUM FALCON
Chewbacca and R2-D2 stay at the flat landing stage where Rey has left the *Millennium Falcon*. Ancient steps lead from here to the interior of the island.

SADDLE
A valley at the top of the ancient set of steps, the saddle provides a breathtaking place for contemplation. This natural amphitheater is where Rey first encounters Luke.

JEDI VILLAGE
These ancient stone structures of unfathomable age were once home to early Jedi. Now, they host Luke and Rey. They are cold huts offering little in the way of comfort.

LUKE SKYWALKER

Intricately woven wool with natural waxes that shed water

SINCE THE FIERY collapse of his Jedi training temple, Luke Skywalker has put that part of his life behind him, focusing instead on the task of living on Ahch-To. In many ways, the toil of his existence on the island mirrors his youth spent on Tatooine. The chores he spent great energy avoiding in his teen years now mark the clock on his long, tiring island days. The native Caretakers pay Luke little mind, for though his spirit is troubled, and his view of the Jedi has clouded, he exhibits no outward ill-will to the island itself and the history it contains. Skywalker has instead respected what island life asks of him, and has carved out a place for himself in this harsh environment.

Pinniped-skin jacket is waterproof

Lowered blast shield

KOENSAYR FLIGHT HELMET WITH BLAST SHIELD

EXILE INTERRUPTED

Luke did not expect Rey's arrival in the *Millennium Falcon*, or for his past to come crashing back into his island life like an ocean wave. He has lost track of time on the island, the result of his willful neglect as well as a mysterious quality the world shares with such Force-infused locales as Dagobah and Mortis. News of the disaster that has befallen the galaxy shocks him out of isolation. The past will not be buried.

MARKSMAN-H TRAINING REMOTE

A PAST LIFE

By a twist of fate, the starship that Rey uses to travel to the island is a flying time capsule of Luke's early adventures, containing the helmet and combat remote he used in his very first Jedi lessons.

Luke's life follows strict routines. In this way, he can efficiently harvest everything he needs from the island, taking advantage of different seasons, times of day, and weather conditions.

Tightly wound leggings

DATA FILE

> Despite living on an island drenched in the Force, Luke has cut off all connection to the mystical energy field.

> Luke was unaware of the fate that befell Han Solo, or of the interstellar cataclysm that wiped out countless lives in the Hosnian system.

ISLAND SURVIVAL

It is no small irony that Luke, who grew up on a parched desert planet, has come to rely on the bounties of the ocean for his survival.

Fishhook made from salvaged wire

FINGERLIP GARPON

TWINFIN HYACANDER

Spear wound

SPETAN CHANNELFISH

Carved bone barbs

SPEARFISHING POLE

Kindling bundle

Breather tank

Empty bottle to collect thala-siren milk

HIKING PACK

Fishing net

WALKING STICK

GROOMING BOX WITH MIRROR

SEALED JUG OF ROE-SALVE

Learning to spearfish during his time on Lew'el, Luke has become adept at using a very long pole that reaches from a bluff and extends into an inlet between opposing cliffs.

Weather shawl

Waterproof boots

LUKE, PREPARED FOR RAIN

LUKE'S HUT

For all its raw beauty, Ahch-To's weather is unpredictable at best, and strong shelter is a necessity. Luke retreats each night to his hut, an ancient corbelled structure made of stacked stones that has stood for millennia. The hut sits in a village built on the southern coast of the island, which is believed to have been the quarters of the earliest Jedi to study on Ahch-To.

Prominent stones point toward local stars

Door made from salvaged S-foil of Luke's T-65 X-wing

LUKE SKYWALKER:
THE LAST JEDI

THE FIRST IN a new era of Jedi Knights, Luke Skywalker took it upon himself to pass on what he had learned. But before restarting the Jedi Order, he had many questions that needed answering. The Empire had expended much effort in eradicating the history of the Jedi, so Skywalker's research into the past was slow and difficult. His questions resulted in a journey that took years, as he chased down every remnant of Jedi lore he could find in an effort to piece together a fragmented past. This quest led Luke to understand much about himself and his destiny, and gave him the confidence needed to revive the Order.

Ahch-To's Jedi temple stands silent and empty. After the fall of Ben Solo, Luke sought to amend for his mistakes by retreating from the Force and the galaxy.

JEDI REKINDLED

Skywalker's first student was to be his sister, Leia. However, she ultimately decided that the best path for her to serve the galaxy left no room for the extended isolation of Jedi training. As Leia concentrated on her new family and senatorial politics, Luke began his travels, largely disappearing from galactic view. During this lengthy journey, Skywalker gathered disciples who would go on to become his first true students.

LUKE'S COMPASS
Recovered from one of the Emperor's observatories on Pillio, this antiquated star compass was among the Jedi relics hoarded by the Emperor during his rule.

Supraluminite lodestone attuned to hyperspace vectors

Hair gray with age and grown long

Luke now only wears this robe to undertake one final Jedi rite

Homespun traditional Jedi robe

> Luke's donning of ceremonial robes is not an indication of a return to faith; rather, Luke sees it as his last rite to end the Order.

> Skywalker's studies revealed the cyclical nature of the struggle between light and dark, and the massive toll the galaxy pays with each cycle.

FLAMES OF FAILURE

Skywalker kept the location of his Jedi training temple a strict secret, known only to members of his burgeoning Order. When he found it ablaze, the grounds littered by slaughtered students, he knew the betrayal came from within. It was his nephew, consumed by darkness, who had led its destruction. The wider galaxy would not know of this calamity for years to come.

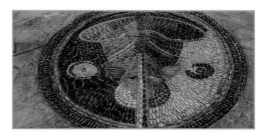

Set into the floor of the Ahch-To temple is an ancient mosaic. According to the Caretakers, it is an image of the Prime Jedi, the first of the Order, in a state of meditation and balance.

JEDI ARTIFACTS

Luke's search for Jedi lore led to him uncovering many lost relics, which he collected and brought with him to Ahch-To. Key to finding the island itself was studying the spread of uneti saplings, a rare type of tree that is sensitive, in its own way, to the Force.

LIGHTNING ROD

Wind indicator

Insulated knurl

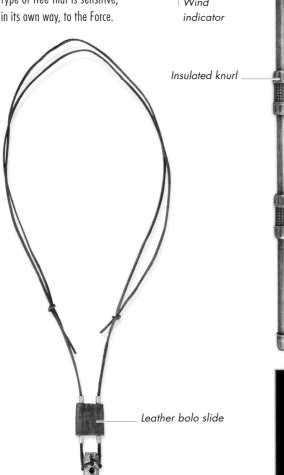

Leather bolo slide

Trophy made from fragmented Sith lightsaber crystal

RECOVERED JEDI CRUSADER PENDANT

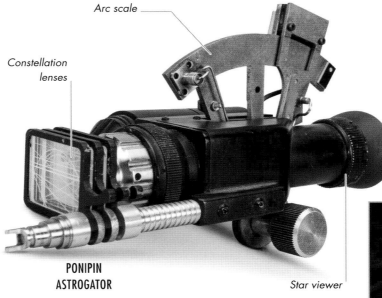

Arc scale

Constellation lenses

Memento salvaged from Luke's crashed X-wing

S-FOIL ACTUATOR CLUTCH DISC

PONIPIN ASTROGATOR

Star viewer

Luke's travels have allowed him to collect and assemble ancient scriptures containing lost Jedi wisdom and abilities. Actual books such as these are a true primitive rarity.

So long and difficult was Rey's journey to find Skywalker that she is taken aback by his refusal to help her. Rey not only seeks Luke to lead the charge against the First Order, she also needs his guidance in understanding and controlling her awakening Force abilities.

REY

Energized plasma blade contained within kyber-generated field

WITH THE FORCE now awakened in Rey, she is filled with newfound ability, insight, and questions. The duel with Kylo Ren on Starkiller Base demonstrated how potent her abilities are when she allows the Force in, but that battle and the events that surrounded it exposed Rey to anger, fear, and aggression—emotions that all too easily lead to the dark side. Rey needs guidance, and there is but one last Jedi Master in the galaxy. When she finds him frustratingly short on answers, Rey does what she does best, and improvises on her own.

Luke refuses Rey's invitation to join her in the Resistance. He turns his back on her, slamming his door in her face. Despite Rey's repeated demands, Luke attempts to ignore her. It becomes a battle of wills, as both Rey and Skywalker are equally stubborn.

Rey has had visions of the island, or at least a place very much like it. Having grown up in the harsh Jakku desert, she found escape through dreams of being surrounded by water. Rather than finding comfort on Ahch-To, however, she is beset by surprises.

REY'S TRAINING

Luke shocks Rey with his view that the time of the Jedi has come to an end. When he finally, with some reluctance, agrees to give her guidance, it comes with many words of warning for the young woman. As Rey's abilities increase, so does a strange and seemingly unprecedented connection in the Force that spans across the galaxy to unite Kylo Ren and Rey. The bond is powerful, and gives Rey insights into Ren that not even Skywalker can see.

Logic function displays

Burtt acoustic signaler

Resistance-issue holster

Leather band across which Rey props her quarterstaff in combat stance

Keeps out the chill of Ahch-To nights

R2-D2
The ever-loyal astromech droid R2-D2 accompanies Rey to Ahch-To, armed with the full navigational data required for the journey. He has not seen Luke Skywalker, his master, in years. R2 longs for him to return, and tries to stir Luke's memories of better days as best he can.

WOVEN BLANKET

Constellations have since changed configuration

Resoled gorvath-wool traveler's boots

ANCIENT STARMAP ARTIFACT

MILLENNIUM FALCON ESCAPE POD

Viewport

Life-support tank

Maneuvering thruster

FACING THE DARKNESS

Rey opens up to the connections of the Force on the island, the web of life that binds all living things. She senses and is drawn to a shadowed area—a gloomy sea cave where the dark side festers. On her own, without Luke's instruction, she visits the cave. Within, her fears and insecurities about her parents, and the reasons why she was abandoned on Jakku manifest themselves. Among the questions that encumber Rey is one of her destiny—what is her role in the conflict that now sweeps the galaxy?

Focused determination and control

Loose open weave tabard in the Jedi tradition

Combat stance learned from years of polearm use

Blade length adjust

Though Han Solo is gone, his reckless spirit lives on. Solo invited Rey onto his crew, and Rey honors that with her continued care of the battered *Falcon*. More than just a pilot and mechanic, Rey finally gets a chance to be a gunner in the ship's ventral turret.

Activation matrix

SKYWALKER'S LIGHTSABER

Built by Anakin Skywalker decades ago, the blue-bladed lightsaber that was once gifted to Luke Skywalker by Obi-Wan Kenobi was thought lost. When it fell into the possession of Maz Kanata, she cared for it, keeping it in operational shape until one day it would point the way to Master Skywalker. But when Rey presents it to Luke, he tosses it aside, hoping to lose it once more.

THE LANAIS

LOCATED ON A NORTHERN INLET on the temple island is a village of natives sworn to their role as Caretakers. These people are the Lanais, and they evolved from the same evolutionary stock of seabirds that produced the unintelligent porgs. Though the Lanais do not appear to possess any exceptional connection to the Force, they do have an uncanny ability to read the intentions of newcomers to the island. Provided that visitors do not intend the island any harm, the Lanais ignore their presence. For thousands of years, the Lanais have tended to the island. Each day, they trek overland to the southern shore, where old Jedi huts are kept in livable condition thanks to their diligence.

The Caretaker duties fall to Lanai females, the more spiritual and empathic members of the species. They keep the stone paths clear of growth, conduct repairs, and prepare meals for the village.

CARETAKERS

The female Lanais are known collectively as the Caretakers, a name derived from their sworn duty to maintain the island. Though they have lived in the shadow of the Jedi temple for millennia, they do not follow the Jedi path. Instead, their own religion has analogues for light and darkness as expressed by the weather of the island. To them, the ideal is a balance in tranquility.

Coarse habit fabric made from woven plant fibers

Tiny placoid scales create rough skin surface

Work apron, washed daily in seawater

TERNA-GENTU, CARETAKER

CLAY CHOPPING BOARD

The Lanais' writing consists of cuneiform marks based on the shape of their feet

FISH-SCALING KNIFE

ALCIDA-AUKA, CARETAKER MATRON
Alcida-Auka is the current leader of the Caretakers, inheriting the position from an untold number of ancestors. She calls the other Caretakers her "daughters," and instills in them the virtues of cleanliness, orderliness, and decorum.

DATA FILE

> Nearly all of the Lanais' technology derives from fish. The bountiful oceans provide a wide variety of aquatic life with useful skins and skeletons.

> The Lanais' language is a combination of spoken words and hand motions. Written language is rare, and fire signals suffice for long-range communications.

VILLAGER TOOLS

To keep rhythm during their repetitive chores, the Lanais' culture is intrinsically musical. Lanai-song is a mix of whistles and guttural oscillations that echo from their village and worksites. The tools of their daily tasks often become impromptu percussion instruments.

Sanded seedpod wash basin

Caudal vertebrae from a tytahuso fish

Pressed waterproof bark strips

Baleen-stripped washboard

WASH BUCKET

WASHSTAND

LADDER

Males and females interact only on a monthly basis, when the males return from the sea, their boats laden with enough fish to feed the village until the next gathering. This multi-day reunion becomes a festival, with music, dance, and food, while long-term romances are rekindled.

Opah-bladder bagpipes

Flotation vest made of vacullacle shells

Dried crinoid frondtrailer hat

Byssus-wool smock

Digitigrade feet

CORM-KAIRUKU, NET-MAKER

HESPER-INGUZA, GUTTER

GREBE-KORORA, PORTER

LANAI INSTRUMENTS

The Lanais' music is loud and boisterous, and includes many folk songs that tell their vast history. Few, if any, feature the Jedi, as if these ancients were somehow above commemorating. Their ballads instead focus on their lives as fishermen and Caretakers.

Billfish beak

ISLAND VISITORS

The male Lanais are known as the Visitors, due to their infrequent presence on the island itself. The males are the hunters and gatherers in the Lanais' society, spending their lives aboard hand-crafted boats that travel the open seas and journey to nearby islands. They return monthly, with hauls of fish that they and the females process for food and tools.

Bioluminescent seeds "sing" when twirled

NIGHTKELP FLAIL

WHARLITHAN HORN

DOUBLE BASS

OPAH-BLADDER BAGPIPES

GNARLGOURD DRUM

AUK-WAIMANU, CAPTAIN

CHEWBACCA

CHEWBACCA'S STRONG protective instincts extend to watching over Rey, especially after the degree to which Han Solo vouched for her. Though Chewie is ever-loyal, he knows better than to crowd a young woman as independent as Rey, who tends to be drawn to isolation. As Rey disappears to follow her duties as a Jedi-in-training, the Wookiee mostly sticks close to the *Millennium Falcon*, forever tinkering with the stubborn freighter, and taking occasional breaks to explore his surroundings on the island.

Keen sense of smell

Leather bandolier with ammunition cases

Wookiee fur consists of three main layers: an outer coat, a mid-fiber layer, and inner down

Rey and Chewbacca soon develop a rhythm as they operate the *Falcon* together. Though a capable pilot himself, Chewie prefers his time-honored role as first mate and copilot, recalibrating the *Falcon's* fickle piloting systems as Rey's instinctive piloting abilities push the ship to its limits.

MILLENNIUM FALCON

Having been separated from the *Falcon* for years as it underwent changes in ownership, Chewbacca takes advantage of every minute of downtime to tear apart access hatches and rediscover the ship's inner workings. He has reset numerous recent "improvements" to the more familiar configurations he and Solo devised years earlier. Complicating this chore is a growing infestation of curious porgs, who have transformed circuit bays into nests.

Mandibles grip containers during cargo-pushing operations

Side-mounted cockpit

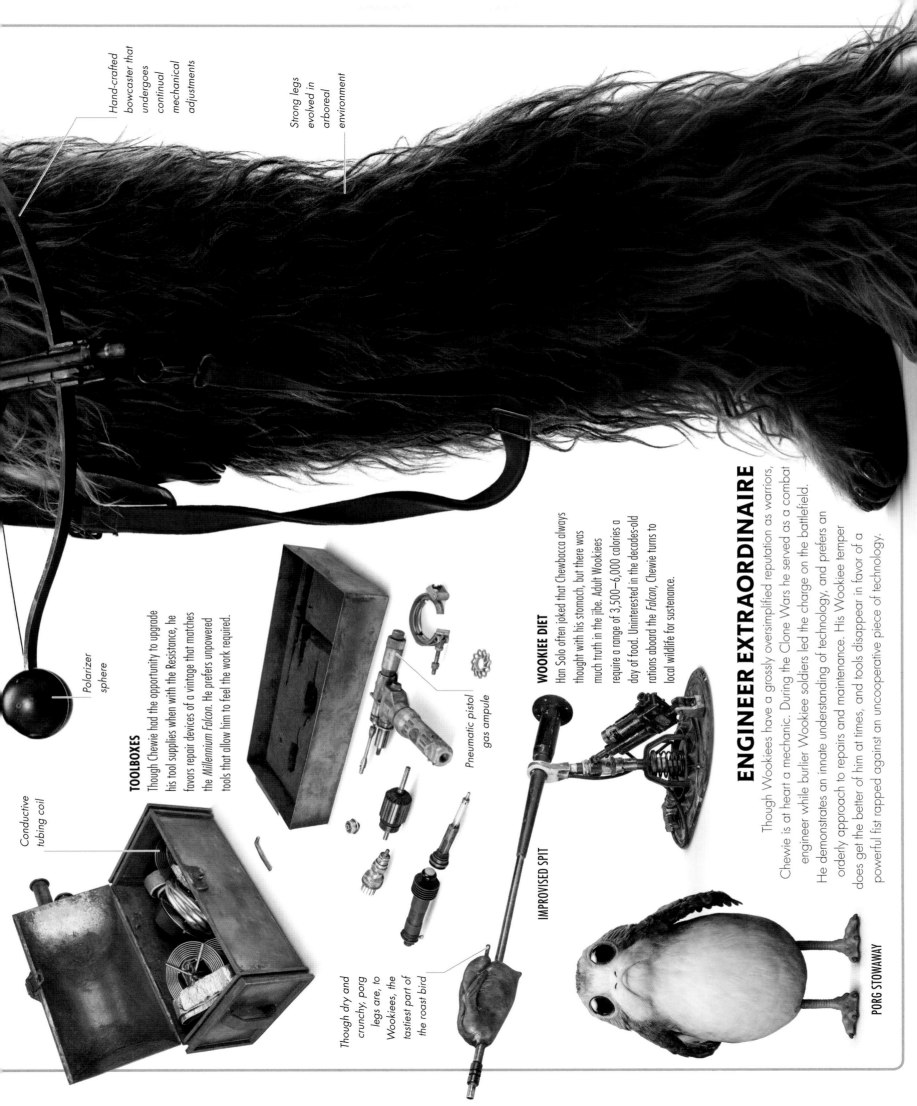

Hand-crafted bowcaster that undergoes continual mechanical adjustments

Strong legs evolved in arboreal environment

Polarizer sphere

Conductive tubing coil

TOOLBOXES

Though Chewie had the opportunity to upgrade his tool supplies when with the Resistance, he favors repair devices of a vintage that matches the *Millennium Falcon*. He prefers unpowered tools that allow him to feel the work required.

Pneumatic pistol gas ampule

Though dry and crunchy, porg legs are, to Wookiees, the tastiest part of the roast bird

IMPROVISED SPIT

WOOKIEE DIET

Han Solo often joked that Chewbacca always thought with his stomach, but there was much truth in the jibe. Adult Wookiees require a range of 3,500–6,000 calories a day of food. Uninterested in the decades-old rations aboard the *Falcon*, Chewie turns to local wildlife for sustenance.

ENGINEER EXTRAORDINAIRE

Though Wookiees have a grossly oversimplified reputation as warriors, Chewie is at heart a mechanic. During the Clone Wars he served as a combat engineer while burlier Wookiee soldiers led the charge on the battlefield. He demonstrates an innate understanding of technology, and prefers an orderly approach to repairs and maintenance. His Wookiee temper does get the better of him at times, and tools disappear in favor of a powerful fist rapped against an uncooperative piece of technology.

PORG STOWAWAY

CANTO BIGHT

AS THE REST OF THE GALAXY falls into conflict, the planet Cantonica and its resort city of Canto Bight remain insulated from the chaos. This does not mean its citizens are unaware of the turmoil gripping the galaxy—rather, these rich barons of industry and commerce see it as an opportunity for immense profit. They have already made fortunes secretly supplying First Order armories. Now that open warfare creates a need for ammunition, technology, and other equipment, these profiteers eagerly foresee the wealth that it will bring.

The Old Town avenues that surround the casino complex are lined with luxury shops that promise a wide variety of rare and bespoke creations. The Raduli café and patisserie on Cabranga Street is a popular eatery.

LUXURY SPEEDERS

Speeder corporations like Astikan Gridworx, SoroSuub Corporation, and Narglatch AirTech make their high-end luxury models available to Cantonica's rich and famous, in hopes of celebrities becoming living advertisements for their products. It's no small irony that those able to afford such speeders rarely need to pay for them.

Discreetly armored power plant

SOLARNOVA TT-86

Formal pointed chauffeur's hat

STREETBOSS 50-50

Ventilation airscoop grill

GROWLER-556

THOMKINS WATAM, CHAUFFEUR

ARRIVING IN STYLE

Guests to the opulent Canto Casino and Racetrack are greeted by valets and hosts who direct them inside without delay. Most guests do not pilot themselves, relying instead on organic chauffeurs who represent a greater status symbol than droid-operated or driverless vehicles. Immense underground parking zones make discreet meeting places for shadowy deals and information exchanges, away from prying eyes.

CASINO ENTRANCE

The tree-lined entryway to the Canto Casino was landscaped at great expense, with rare Alderaanian chinar trees engineered from a private seed bank.

Glove fitted with concealed pocket to deliver bribes

Ostentatious vessels such as the *Undisputed Victor*—captained by Baron Yasto Attsmun, a tyrant from Listehol—voyage across the resort's artificial sea. The baron's attempts to woo nightclub owner Ubialla Gheal meet with little success.

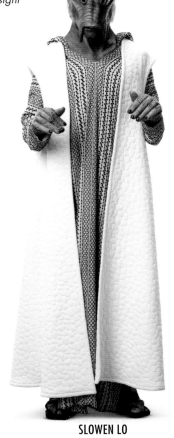

Surgical implant lenses amplify failing eyesight

SLOWEN LO

Canto Bight local Slowen Lo has made a fortune selling driftwood sculptures, and now owns a beachside residence. He is concerned about a shuttle seemingly abandoned on the beach, and reports it to the Canto Bight Police Department.

BRONZIUM MINERAL- OIL PITCHER

FATHIER-BRISTLE SKIN BRUSH

RINSING BOWL

Chemically sensitive receptors can detect lactic acid in body tissue

Necklace contains translator to allow communication with varied clientele

Fingertips can create soothing vibrations

LEXO SOOGER, MASSEUR

Kedpin Shoklop has been looking forward to a relaxing massage at Zord's. Lucky Shoklop won a two-week trip to Canto Bight.

SPA TREATMENTS

The city's visitors and residents treat themselves to indulgent spa sessions in order to offset the "stresses" of their wealth and power. Zord's Spa and Bathhouse in Old Town offers a wide assortment of pampering amenities, including zero-gravity massagers, ozone chambers, medicated rinses, mud tanks, and gill-flushes. Zord's Spa leaves its customers in the capable hands of skilled specialists rather than entrusting them to impersonal droids.

STURG GANNA

Ticklish tail end, considered off-limits

Heat-retaining stone plinth

CANTO BIGHT POLICE

PUBLIC SAFETY is taken seriously in Canto Bight, for secure visitors are generous visitors. Society is tiered here, with the wealthiest having the greatest sense of security and immediate access to justice—a flexible concept in Canto Bight. Every law and regulation in this city is negotiable, depending on the wealth of the suspect or accuser. Corruption is rampant in law enforcement, and as long as transgressions do not disrupt the resort's relaxing atmosphere, much can be ignored. Nonetheless, there are unspoken rules, and lines that should not be crossed.

The veneer of this coastal city is carefully and expensively maintained. Property crime is not tolerated here, and offenses such as vandalism or even littering are punished with greater severity on Cantonica than on most other planets.

POLICE GLOW ROD

Glow rod can double as crude baton

Multi-spectrum illuminator array for crime scene investigation

Fineweave cape

PATROL COPS

The most visible members of the Canto Bight Police Department (CBPD) are the Uniformed Branch. These officers patrol the Old Town and casino grounds looking for troublemakers and projecting a general air of order and efficiency. Hospitality training is part of the CBPD academy curriculum, as keeping guests content is the key to keeping them docile. The police headquarters is also the site of the largest jail on Cantonica.

Holographic department letters can reverse for rearview mirror legibility

OFFICER SOMMEL ATANDU

High-impact betaplast flexible neck guard

POLICE SPEEDER

Anyone attempting to evade the law in Canto Bight had best move fast, as police employ swift, lightweight GB-134 pursuit craft, also known as jet-sticks. The nimble craft are well suited to navigating the narrow roadways of the Old Town.

CBMP (Canto Bight Mounted Police) officer with flight goggles

Noise suppression and range-extending barrel attachment

Rank insignia

Betaplast armored collar

Control pedal

SCRAMBLED LONG-RANGE COMLINK

Multi-setting laser cannon

ELECTRO-SHOCK STUN PROD

Repulsorlift generator forks

NON-LETHAL FORCE

The police are trained to subdue and arrest without resorting to lethal force, in an effort to maintain the confidence and comfort of the public. Even the slightest injury suffered by a bystander or a suspect could have costly legal and public-relations consequences. Officers' blaster weaponry is set to stun by default, and patrols carry electro-shock stun prods to deal with tough targets. Since weapons are prohibited in public areas, firefights in Canto Bight are rare.

Short-range wrist comlink

DATA FILE

> The Canto Bight police headquarters stands on a hill above the Old Town, giving the officers in its surveillance center a clear view of events unfolding in the streets below.

Additional ammunition reservoir in stock

Attached glow rod

RELBY K-25 BLASTER (RIFLE CONFIGURATION)

Long-range macroscope

RELBY K-25 BLASTER (DEFAULT CONFIGURATION)

RELBY K-25 BLASTER (HEAVY CONFIGURATION)

High-polish synth-hide officer's boots

OFFICER STEPHEDEN THALDREE

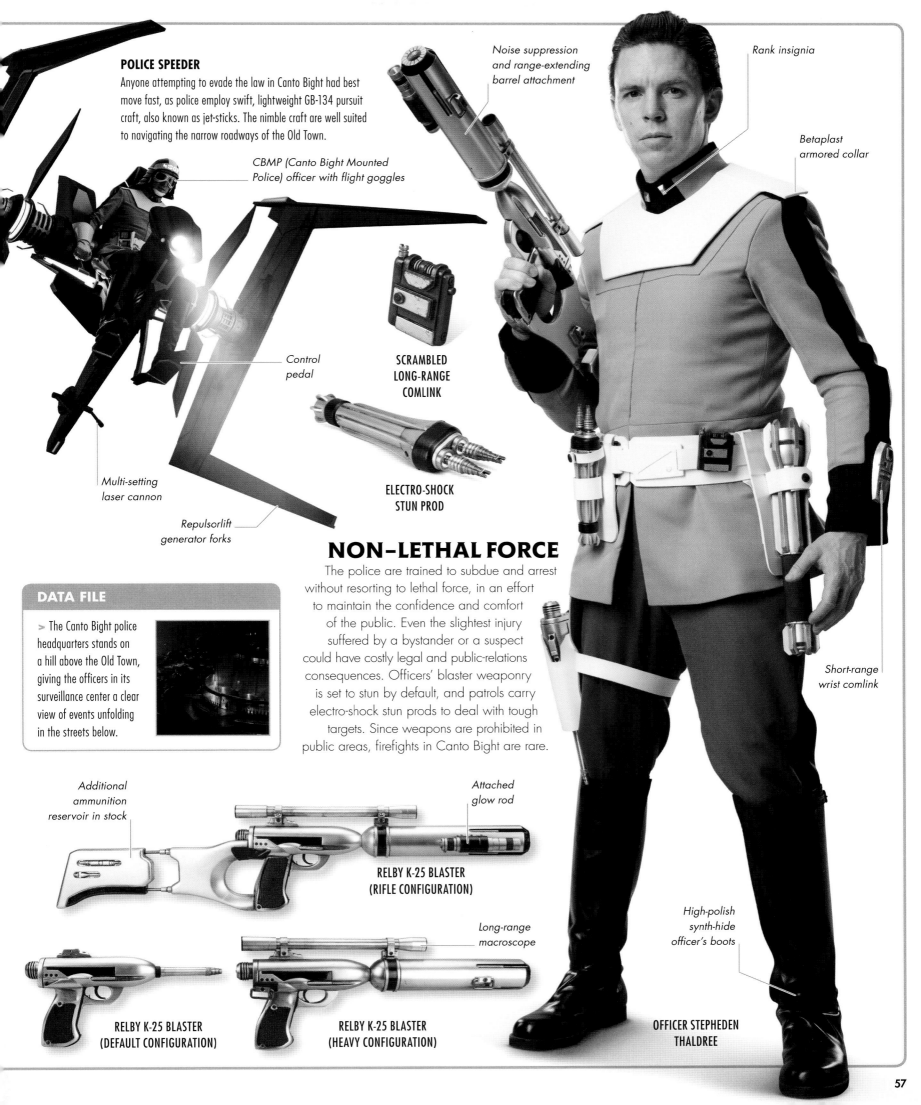

THE CASINO

SEPARATING CENTRAL OLD TOWN from the artificial coastline is the massive Canto Casino and Racetrack, a structure whose activities dominate the days and nights of Canto Bight. This complex includes a luxury hotel, a number of top-rated restaurants, a shopping concourse, and bustling game rooms that overlook the fathier racetrack. Cantonica favors its own currency, made from precious aurodium, rather than relying on the volatile value of New Republic credits. Visitors looking to spend money in the casino must exchange their funds for the resort standard.

The casino's interiors match the sandy hue of the planet's original desert environment. Sweeping curved walls and ceilings are adorned with gleaming fixtures and stained glass windows.

AT THE TABLES

The games of chance at the Canto Casino are more upscale than common amusements found in spaceport cantinas. Sabacc, binspo, and dejarik are frowned upon in favor of "gentlebeing's games," such as Savareen Whist, Zinbiddle, Uvide, and the ever-popular Hazard Toss, which is sure to draw a crowd when a gambler hits a winning streak.

SOBURI HANNEMTIN, CROUPIER

Vest in casino livery

Hand signals let bouncers communicate silently

Fierce expression; the only casino employees permitted to scowl

Smartly tailored jacket conceals stun baton

KUARI ZINBIDDLE CARDS

A Vermilion Six is needed for an "Ion Barrage" hand

Shimmersilk cummerbund hides comlink

ROLLING CUP

HAZARD TOSS DICE

PEMMIN BRUNCE

CASINO SECURITY
While the CBPD can be called in to handle major disturbances in the casino, the everyday guarding of the venue is carried out by plainclothed bouncers who report to head of security, Pemmin Brunce.

The audience cheers as Sosear Latta, a lesser count, scores a perfect cross-cap in Hazard Toss. The table's croupier, Karlus Stee, keeps a sharp eye open for any cheating, but so far everything seems clean.

Polished dress shoes

GAMING MACHINES

For those looking to gamble at their own pace, the casino has carousels of floating slot machines. Gamers feed coins into the slots, causing the trio of reels to spin, and hope that they display a row of matching symbols once they come to a stop.

Coin input slot

Center symbol reel

Bonus and game status display

Payout tray

Repulsorlifts in base

Quantum-layered carbonite shell prevents tampering

THAMM

Thamm is currently the most popular croupier on the gambling hall floor. His boisterous demeanor is encouraging to nervous gamblers, while his consoling nature helps cushion devastating losses. The tiny quadruped exudes an oddly pleasing aroma that helps put patrons at ease.

CROUPIER STICK

Illuminated indicators change color to denote drink specials

PRECIOUS METAL CANTOCOINS

Inner edge has magnetic strips to better gather coins

Tentacular embouchure

F'nonc horn gas bag

HHEX

Wide-set eyes

Traditional yekermo outer robes

SE8 WAITER DROID

Industrial Automaton SE8 servant droids shuffle across the casino, weaving their way through crowds to deliver refreshments to discerning customers.

DATA FILE

> The casino favors dice games as they are harder to cheat at, though this doesn't stop some from trying.

> Sophisticated sensors constantly scan the casino for electronic or quantum-based cheating devices.

THE BAND

Jhat, Dhuz, and Hhex are wind instrument players from a naturally musical species, the Palandags, who communicate through musical sounds of different pitches. Their powerful exolungs make them the galaxy's leading f'nonc horn performers.

CASINO GUESTS

THE CANTO CASINO CLIENTELE is a mixture of many kinds of beings, all with one thing in common—they have the money necessary to play the high-stakes games. Politicians, celebrities, and above all, business magnates gather to play and make deals away from public scrutiny. These revelers are insulated from the daily lives of other galactic citizens by their unfathomable wealth. That their profit-making may cause suffering to others is of no interest to the galaxy's elite.

WINNING THREE
The trio of Wodibin, Thodibin, and Dodibin belong to an eerily lucky species, the Suertons, who appear to have the ability to subconsciously affect probability. They are closely monitored by casino security, but the "Winning Three" seem devoid of malevolence. These light-hearted beings care more about having fun than wealth.

Distinctive white streak (artificial)

Gaberwool tuxedo coat

Nova Sundari-style hairdo

Serendibite earrings

Stellabora lapel bloom

Formal coat

CODEBREAKER'S PLATINUM RING

Fitted lattice dress with low clarion skirt

"LOVEY"

Matching Master Codebreaker's level of secrecy, his companion refuses to tell him her real name—so he simply calls her "Lovey."

DODIBIN

Dress shoes have hidden compartments

MASTER CODEBREAKER
Known only by his intriguing title, Master Codebreaker keeps his real identity a secret. He has posted his personal data in a public network node, wrapped in quantum-spread biohexacrypt code. It is an open invitation: Anyone who can crack his code is welcome to take over the mantle of Master Codebreaker. To date, no one has come close. The Canto Casino only lets the Codebreaker play dice games, and forbids him from any electronic forms of entertainment.

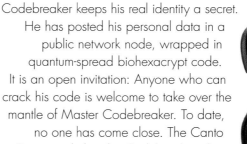

THE ELITE

It is a mark of special social status to enter the exclusive, innermost clubs within the Canto Casino. Annual private parties stir up heated demand to get on the guest list, and past guests make exceptional efforts to remain relevant each passing year. Baroness Tagge-Simoni, for instance, is too frail and aged to attend in person, but appears as a young holographic head projected from a droid body.

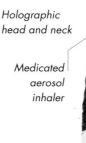

Holographic head and neck

Medicated aerosol inhaler

EDMO ECTACLE

SOSEAR LATTA

DEFANCIO STORSILT

CENTADA RESSAD

RHOMBY AND PARALLELA GRAMMUS

Wealth attracts eccentrics, and the Grammus sisters are among the most striking in the city. These identical performance artists claim to be from another dimension, and sometimes speak in a seemingly invented language.

BARONESS WAYULIA TAGGE-SIMONI

Thick, puncture-proof outer skin

The Onyx Bands of Cato Neimoidia

TRYPTO BUBALL

THE COUNTESS

Contessa Alissyndrex delga Cantonica Provincion (or more simply, the Countess of Canto Bight) is of royal blood and nominally presides over the city. Her husband, the Count, is rarely seen in public.

Freshly exfoliated face

Self-spun web-chiffon drape

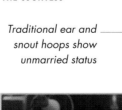

BUBALL'S CANE

Engorged egg sac

NEEPERS PANPICK

Traditional ear and snout hoops show unmarried status

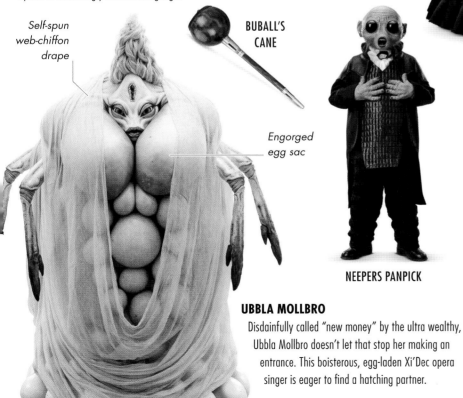

UBBLA MOLLBRO

Disdainfully called "new money" by the ultra wealthy, Ubbla Mollbro doesn't let that stop her making an entrance. This boisterous, egg-laden Xi'Dec opera singer is eager to find a hatching partner.

Snook Uccorfay is a raconteur who lives life to the fullest, in order to build a catalog of outlandish tales. He is drawn like a tractor beam to wealthy females, and dazzles them all with his exceptional dancing.

SNOOK UCCORFAY

FATHIERS

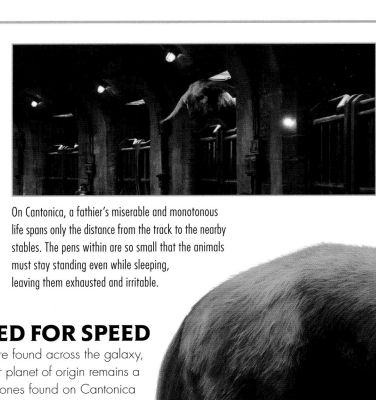

FORTUNES ARE WON and lost on the backs of the racing fathiers of Canto Bight. These graceful steeds are bred and trained to maximize their speed and power, to the delight of their wealthy spectators. The pageantry and raw power of the sport conceals an unpleasant reality—these majestic animals are penned in tight quarters, frequently beaten, and are pushed to the limits of their endurance in the name of entertainment. Attempts to regulate or outright ban the sport have failed. There is simply too much greed involved to stop the races.

On Cantonica, a fathier's miserable and monotonous life spans only the distance from the track to the nearby stables. The pens within are so small that the animals must stay standing even while sleeping, leaving them exhausted and irritable.

Identification chevron

Sponsor logo emblazoned on helmet

PINRADO NOZA

Padded wrist guards

SHUMA KALAMO

ARCA YROCA

BRED FOR SPEED

Fathiers are found across the galaxy, although their planet of origin remains a mystery. The ones found on Cantonica are bred specifically for speed and endurance. Their builds are lean, and their metabolisms are high and hot-blooded. Their powerful legs propel the massive animals to speeds upwards of 75 kilometers per hour, while their long, wing-like ears help dissipate excess body heat and act as air-steering rudders.

High cantle holds jockey in position

RACING SADDLE

Shape minimizes air resistance

Hock joint undergoes immense strain when running or jumping

HIGH-IMPACT HELMET

FATHIER JOCKEYS

The skill of the jockeys separates prize-winners from also-rans, but it is a risky profession: Falls are often fatal. Most races in Canto Bight are flat races—without jumps—meaning that raw speed is the ultimate factor in victories. Fathiers do not have the endurance to run at full speed across the entire race, so jockeys must apply force for bursts of speed when it can be most impactful.

ELECTROCROP

JOCKEY EQUIPMENT

Fathier jockey gear is built to reduce weight and air drag. Sleek lycresh fabric envelopes the rider in a comfortable fit, usually finished with bright, attention-grabbing colors.

DATA FILE

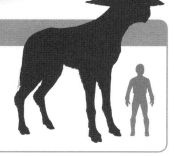

> Those who have never seen a fathier in person are often shocked by their true size. The average fathier stands 3 meters high at the shoulder.

Ears have dense
blood vessels
near surface to
assist in cooling

Wide binocular
field of vision

BARGWILL
TOMDER

Infected
ingrown
nose
tendrils

Nose length can
be deciding factor
in close races

Looped
dressage
whip

Four dexterous
arms typical of
Cloddograns

THE STABLES

Managing the fathiers is the surly groom Bargwill Tomder.
He oversees a small team of urchins—children abandoned
on Cantonica by losing gamblers—whose small size
assists in navigating the cramped confines of the stables.
Tomder is ill-tempered, and his default approach to
solving problems is simply to crack his whip.

Powerful
forearm
muscles

As children do all across the galaxy, the stable
hands engage in imaginative play to fill their
downtime. Travelers from distant worlds
bring them fragmented tales of adventure
that excite their young imaginations.

Unlock switch

FATHIER BRUSH

STABLE DOOR CONTROL

Serrated
hoof pick

Farrier rasp

Collapsible
glow rod

JEDI DOLL

WALKER TOY

Rough work
boots

Keratinized
hoof absorbs
gallop impact

ARASHELL SAR

TEMIRI BLAGG

ONIHO ZAYA

GANGSTER DOLL

"DJ"

EVEN IN THE MOST luxurious heights dwell lowly thieves. On the rare occasion that he feels compelled to excuse his actions, the man known as DJ claims to be a victim of society's imbalance, which tips all odds toward the wealthy. Although DJ prides himself on not being trapped by riches, he does covet money. As far as he's concerned, getting your hands on currency, no matter how, means you've earned it. The galaxy is filled with con artists, but DJ insists he's the only one honest enough to openly acknowledge what he wants, and just how far he'll go to get it.

"DON'T JOIN" HAT PLATE

Tin plate with stamped "DON'T JOIN" warning

Skin left unwashed for several days

Well-worn work boots

Ring with amber from Trammis III

DJ has won and lost countless credits, but he weathers his constantly changing fortunes with an armor of cynicism. He is an opportunistic survivor, who will do or say anything to con another day.

Modified Zinbiddle card infected with custom slicer virus

Liquid-metal teeth automatically change shape to match lock

SKELETON KEY

DJ has incredible technical aptitude and a knack for cryptography. He handcrafts his own computer spikes and bypass keys capable of temporarily befuddling even bio-hexacrypt-protected data networks. If he had the discipline, he could excel in the information security industries.

Kodyok-leather coat

DON'T JOIN

DJ has little that passes as a personal ethos, save for the two words that are the source of his nickname: DON'T JOIN. He thinks larger causes are for fools, since society is just a machine looking to turn everyone into a cog. First Order, Resistance, or New Republic—it doesn't matter where on the spectrum such a cause may lie, ultimately all are meat grinders that chew up their followers with the same disinterest.

THE *LIBERTINE*

DJ steals the *Libertine* in order to depart from Cantonica. The sleek star yacht belongs to a manager with the Sienar-Jaemus corporation, who has been making a tidy profit selling surplus starfighters to independent worlds nervously expecting a new galactic war. DJ feels no qualms stealing such a prize, as he figures its original owner is just as corrupt as he is.

Recessed sublight drive

Communications spine

Repulsorlift generator plane

DJ finds comfort in the *Libertine*'s luxurious interior. He quickly bypasses locks granting him access to the ship's safe, liquor cabinet, and computer systems. Inside its databanks, he finds a catalog of starfighters for sale.

CANTO BIGHT JAIL

Already known to local authorities, DJ purposely arranges his own arrest for a petty crime. The jail is the only place he can grab some sleep with the assurance that he won't be pestered by the Canto Bight Police Department.

Illegal x-ray monocle

JIO LOSTER

Guavian Death Gang jacket

Airspeeder jacket

Data goggles

Helmet with tracking sensors

Welding tank (empty)

OLVIN TEEPS

TORREB SAVATO

WOLFID DORNA

DAXO "ODDS" ECLOSS

OTHER PRISONERS

The free-flowing wealth in Canto Bight attracts all manner of thieves and pickpockets, who find to their dismay that the locals pay well for security. Those who underestimate the CBPD will find themselves cooling down in the local prison. Criminals are able to work off their fines and sentences through menial labor in Cantonica's industrial and infrastructure services.

INFILTRATION

Crested officer's cap with First Order emblem

Rank cylinders (blank and unregistered)

WITH TIME TICKING AWAY for the Resistance fleet, Finn and Rose take advantage of DJ's code-cracking skills to sneak onto Snoke's Mega-Destroyer. Soon, the infiltrators are disguised as First Order officers—with varying degrees of success. Their objective: to reach and disable the hyperspace tracker long enough to allow the Resistance fleet a single, unmonitored lightspeed jump. Hurriedly navigating the enormous interior of the *Supremacy* while attempting to remain inconspicuous proves to be a challenge. Finn's inside knowledge of the flagship's layout is invaluable, but vigilant troopers, officers, and droids await at every turn, of which there are many.

TRAITOR'S RETURN

Finn is more than passingly familiar with Snoke's immense warship. As part of his service aboard the *Finalizer*, Finn spent several brief stints on the *Supremacy* as his Star Destroyer underwent servicing within the Mega-Destroyer's enormous docks. This included uneventful rotation through shifts of guard, inspection, sanitation, and gunnery duties. Finn returns, fearing that his reputation as the only stormtrooper to break ranks may precede him. Raiding a laundry room, he dons the uniform of a nameless captain.

SECURITY-SEALED OFFICER'S DATAPAD

FIRST ORDER BINDERS

DATA FILE

> DJ's code creates a gap in the *Supremacy*'s sensor perimeter, letting the *Libertine* land in a heat-sink structure hidden in the glow of an immense engine.

> Unable to procure working code cylinders in the laundry room, Finn has to guide the team on a path to the tracking room that bypasses major security checkpoints.

LAUNDRY DROID

Tending the uniforms of the First Order aboard the *Supremacy* are thousands of Serv-O-Droid SO-1P autovalet droids. These menial, fifth-degree automatons have little personality programming, and are solely dedicated to the washing, folding, and upkeep of military linens.

Sensors detect fabric type

Steam iron

Pressing surface with inlaid drying vacuums

Officer's cap in
major's colors

Rose has
bypassed the
security locks on
her blaster pistol

DROID IN DISGUISE

BB-8 is hard to hide in the open, however a crude but effective disguise is improvised by simply emptying a garbage can, inverting it, and using it to cover the little droid.

High-security
access keys

Quick-draw
shoulder holster

FIRST ORDER SECURITY BUREAU

Loyalty to the First Order is drummed into personnel throughout their lives, ensured by the efforts of the First Order Security Bureau. Agents, observers, loyalty officers, and others closely watch the crews for any transgressions, hoping to prevent another desertion with disastrous consequences like FN-2187's infamous betrayal.

Tipped off by BB-9E, Colonel Garmuth gathers stormtroopers and alerts Captain Phasma of the infiltration. Garmuth intends to make a very public display of capturing and eliminating the traitor and his ally.

INSIDE THE MONSTER'S DEN

In other circumstances, Rose would marvel at the impressive technological advancements on display all around her, but her focus on the Resistance mission is unbreakable. Disguised as a major, Rose is not used to the pressed and tidy officer's uniform, preferring instead the far more comfortable baggy work coveralls of a Resistance technician. However, she plays the role well enough that a junior officer seeks her approval, little suspecting that Rose is not what she seems.

COLONEL
ANSIV GARMUTH

Ill-fitting,
uncomfortable
boots

Crates filled with
payoff money on
repulsor pallet

BLOOD MONEY

The First Order's plunder of worlds in its domain has filled its coffers with local currencies minted from precious metals. These peggats, aurei, and zemids have universal value as they can be melted down.

CAPTAIN PHASMA

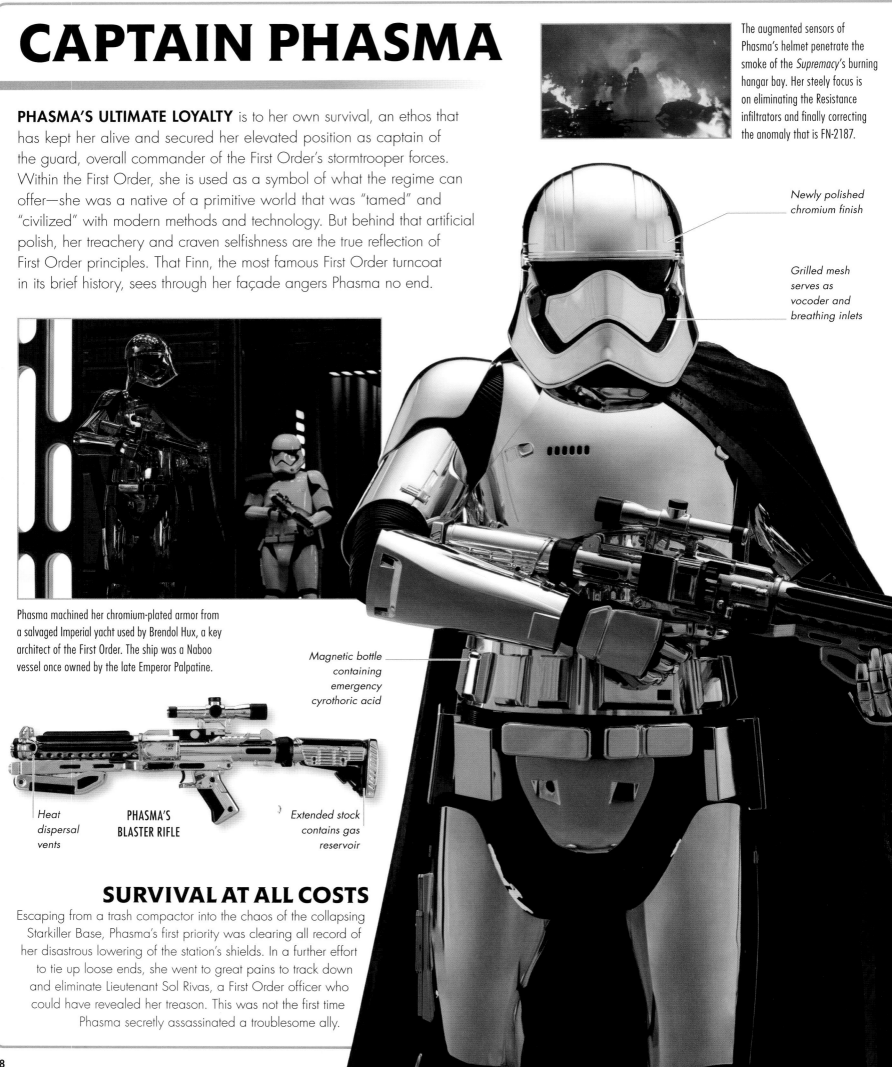

PHASMA'S ULTIMATE LOYALTY is to her own survival, an ethos that has kept her alive and secured her elevated position as captain of the guard, overall commander of the First Order's stormtrooper forces. Within the First Order, she is used as a symbol of what the regime can offer—she was a native of a primitive world that was "tamed" and "civilized" with modern methods and technology. But behind that artificial polish, her treachery and craven selfishness are the true reflection of First Order principles. That Finn, the most famous First Order turncoat in its brief history, sees through her façade angers Phasma no end.

The augmented sensors of Phasma's helmet penetrate the smoke of the *Supremacy*'s burning hangar bay. Her steely focus is on eliminating the Resistance infiltrators and finally correcting the anomaly that is FN-2187.

Newly polished chromium finish

Grilled mesh serves as vocoder and breathing inlets

Phasma machined her chromium-plated armor from a salvaged Imperial yacht used by Brendol Hux, a key architect of the First Order. The ship was a Naboo vessel once owned by the late Emperor Palpatine.

Magnetic bottle containing emergency cyrothoric acid

Heat dispersal vents

PHASMA'S BLASTER RIFLE

Extended stock contains gas reservoir

SURVIVAL AT ALL COSTS

Escaping from a trash compactor into the chaos of the collapsing Starkiller Base, Phasma's first priority was clearing all record of her disastrous lowering of the station's shields. In a further effort to tie up loose ends, she went to great pains to track down and eliminate Lieutenant Sol Rivas, a First Order officer who could have revealed her treason. This was not the first time Phasma secretly assassinated a troublesome ally.

HELMET INTERFACE

Phasma's armor has custom modifications that give her an advantage in combat. Behind her helmet's tempered, polarized lenses is an upgraded integral MFTAS (Multi-Frequency Targeting Acquisition System). This cuts through low light and atmospheric interference.

Blue eyes hidden by expressionless mask

DATA FILE

> Phasma used an anti-armor acidic compound to dissolve the door of the Starkiller trash compactor into which she was dumped.

> Phasma and Hux have conspired in the elimination of mutual political rivals.

MODIFIED CRUSHGAUNTS

Chromium-plated carbon barrel head

Sight housing

SE-44C BLASTER PISTOL (CUSTOMIZED)

Grip encoded to Phasma's biosignature

Quicksilver baton in active mode

Armorweave cape denotes status as captain of the guard

QUICKSILVER BATON

Phasma wields a quicksilver baton for close combat. The durable cylinder is made from a collapsible micromesh matrix held in a containment field. When inactive, it condenses down to a small baton. When active, it instantly expands to its full length.

Field-shaped spearpoint never dulls

CLOSE COMBAT

Phasma grew up in the wilds of Parnassos, a harsh world of unforgiving terrain and weather. Born of a tribe that dwelled in the jagged rocks of the Scyre, Phasma lived a merciless kill-or-be-killed existence. When the First Order came to her world, she saw an opportunity to escape that life by cementing her loyalty to the powerful off-worlders, and abandoned her people to become a high-tech soldier. Her skill with traditional melee weapons is a marker of her primitive past.

Segmented sabatons, newly polished by low-ranking troops

STORMTROOPERS

THE ARMORED SOLDIERS of the First Order are the latest evolution of one of the galaxy's most distinctive symbols of military might: the stormtrooper. That the First Order had stormtroopers in its ranks was no secret to the New Republic, even though, strictly speaking, they were forbidden by the Galactic Concordance treaty. That they were more than a defense force and actually an invasion army is what few outside of the Resistance predicted. For the young men and women beneath the helmets, this is their moment in history. They have trained a lifetime to serve one purpose—using strength to bring order to chaos.

High-density ammunition power cells

Composite betaplast armor

FWMB-10 megablaster

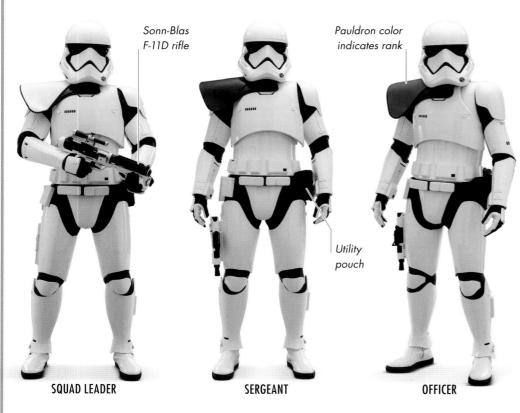

Sonn-Blas F-11D rifle

Pauldron color indicates rank

Utility pouch

SQUAD LEADER **SERGEANT** **OFFICER**

HEAVY TROOPER

Additional specialist gear diversifies the stormtrooper ranks, giving commanding officers greater options when deploying forces. The heavy trooper specialist carries web gear loaded with extra ammunition, designed to power the megablaster squad assault weapon he or she carries.

SECRETS UNCOVERED

In his brief time at Resistance headquarters, Finn provided his newfound allies with valuable intelligence on the stormtrooper program. Though Finn's low rank limited the scope of his knowledge, he nonetheless was able to confirm a number of rumors. That the First Order draws stormtrooper cadets as children from conquered worlds is a firsthand experience for Finn. This strategy is an evolution of a training regimen originally devised by the late Imperial general Brendol Hux.

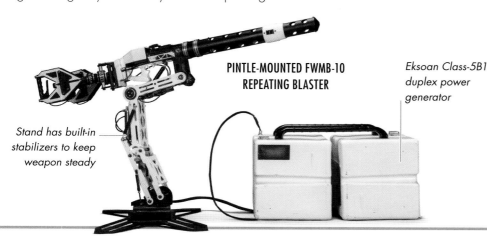

PINTLE-MOUNTED FWMB-10 REPEATING BLASTER

Eksoan Class-5B1 duplex power generator

Stand has built-in stabilizers to keep weapon steady

The standard operational unit for stormtroopers is the squad, made up of ten troopers. It is common for squadmates to have trained together in large classes called batches— Finn trained under Batch Eight, which has graduates stationed aboard the *Supremacy*.

EXECUTIONER TROOPER

The First Order shows its intolerance of disloyalty with regular public executions. Executioner troopers are not drawn from a specialist infantry unit. Rather, it is a role that any standard stormtrooper may find him or herself in, based on that day's assignments. The willingness to carry out capital punishment without hesitation is a mark of effective stormtrooper training.

Collimator sleeve

Polarized lenses with multi-frequency targeting and acquisition system (MFTAS)

Carbon-finish armor denotes executioner role

LASER AX
Executioner troopers carry weapons that maximize the theatricality of First Order justice. The laser ax is a powered hand weapon with a quartet of collapsible claws, from which extend razor-sharp energy ribbons.

Emitter claws (in stowed configuration)

Monomolecular energy ribbon with cycling power

Extended emitter claws

Temperature control body glove

EXECUTIONER HELMET
Executioner troopers wear custom-marked armor to denote their duty. Unlike standard armor, which broadcasts a trooper's serial number to their squadmates' helmet displays, executioner armor is silent in regards to identity, leaving the executioner anonymous to all but their commanding officer.

Vocodor can further disguise identity with voice modulation

Betaplast knee plate

Flexible weatherproof boots

DATA FILE

> Stormtroopers do not have individual names, and are identified only by serial numbers.

> Not all stormtroopers are aware of Finn's defection, suggesting that word of his disloyalty has been suppressed to prevent it from inspiring others.

CRAIT

THE LAST GASP of hope for the Resistance is the otherwise uninviting mineral planet of Crait, tucked in a remote sector of the Outer Rim Territories. This has been Leia Organa and Amilyn Holdo's secret endgame—bunkering down on a former rebel world that had fallen off most modern starcharts. The Resistance's penchant for using old rebel-era caches and facilities is part of Leia's strategy, for she alone has a store of navigational information from the early days of the Rebellion that she has never shared.

Resistance U-55 loadlifter evacuation transports crowd into the gloom of the abandoned mine, the number of surviving personnel steadily dwindling as they rush out to repel the First Order's tenacious assault.

Transparisteel windows offer panoramic views

BlasTech hepta-mag ammunition carrier belt

Rank markings on helmet

Duty uniform identification plaque

RESISTANCE TRANSPORTS

Sienar Fleet Systems U-55 loadlifters, outdated yet still functional craft, are versatile orbital ferries designed for a variety of functions. These transports are commonly known as lifeboats to the Resistance personnel that crowd aboard them, and that is indeed their function during the dramatic escape to Crait's surface.

Lenses filter out atmospheric dust and haze

NEURO-SAAV ND.621 RANGEFINDER

KOO MILLHAM, GROUND LOGISTICS DIVISION

Flame-resistant material

FINAL EVACUATION

With the fleet exhausted of fuel by the lengthy pursuit, the surviving Resistance crew brave the landing on Crait with the First Order still at their heels. Now numbering only in the dozens, the evacuees must bravely stage a holding action long enough for Leia Organa's distress call to be answered. Though their position is fortified, it is clear this may be their last stand. If the defenses fall, then there will be no one left to continue the struggle.

COVA NELL, TRANSPORT PILOT

SERGEANT "SALTY" SHARP

> Crait's day lasts 27 standard hours. It orbits its star (also named Crait) in 525 standard days.

> Crait's breathable atmosphere comes from the slow dissolving of subterranean solid oxygen and nitrogen-suspending crystalline compounds.

DESOLATE WORLD

The Resistance fleet crawls at sublight speed toward this moonless, highly reflective planet. Crait's surface is covered in barren salt flats, with steppes of halite breaking up the terrain. Just beneath the salt is a thick crust of red crystalline rhodochrosite—a moderately valuable commodity. An underground briny ocean seeps through the softer minerals, creating an enormous cave network.

The Nupayuni salt flats, named after the original mining charter

MINE BASE

The Nupayuni Mining Consortium charted Crait decades ago as a potential excavation planet. The enterprise was abandoned shortly afterward, but early construction efforts erected an enormous blast door to withstand blistering crystalstorms as well as rare but titanic wildlife. The Mining Guild simply abandoned its equipment rather than pay for its salvage, and rebel engineers made further modifications, adding a localized bombardment shield.

BASE DEFENSES

The Rebellion hastily abandoned Crait during the base's construction when a traitorous ally alerted an elite Imperial unit, SCAR Squadron, to their location. The rebels left behind their Spiezoc v-120 and v-232 artillery emplacements.

Keen eyesight adapted to low light conditions

Sharp crystalline "fur" evolved as a defense mechanism

Whiskers help a vulptex navigate darkened tunnels

BLASTER RIFLE RECHARGING BACKPACK

HORIZON-RANGE COMMS ANTENNA

Targeting data input

VULPTEX

Since its abandonment decades earlier, the mine base has become home to a skulk of vulptices—fox-like creatures with crystalline features. The curious vulptices have explored the deepest depths of the caverns, finding pathways that only they can traverse.

PORTABLE BATTLE ANALYSIS COMPUTER

FIRST ORDER INVASION

WHEN PURSUIT of the Resistance turns from an interstellar chase into asymmetric ground combat, the First Order continues to dominate with its intimidating armored forces. Proving the cyclical nature of history, the Battle of Crait recasts ancient siege tactics with modern battlefield technology. Newly designed colossal combat walkers plod overland to root out the entrenched Resistance.

AT–M6

The All Terrain MegaCaliber Six (AT-M6) walker is effectively a towering mobile artillery cannon. Over 36 meters tall, the AT-M6 has a hunched build and a knuckle-walking gait similar to that seen in simians. The heavy legs and finger-like structures are designed to secure purchase and stabilize the massively powerful turbolaser on its back.

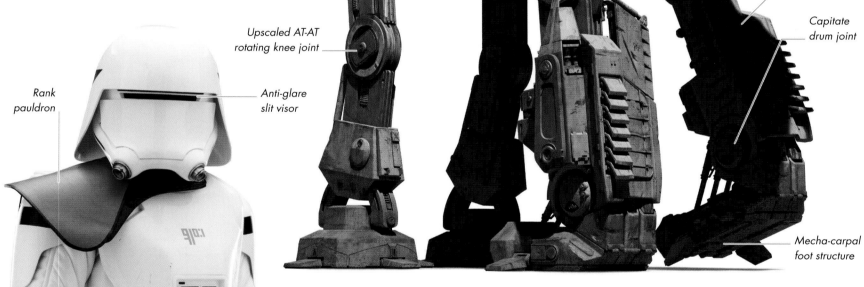

Ultra-dense matrixed composite armor

MegaCaliber Six turbolaser cannon

Armored crew cabin

Heavy fire-linked dual laser cannons

Reinforced forward leg armor

Capitate drum joint

Mecha-carpal foot structure

Upscaled AT-AT rotating knee joint

Rank pauldron

Anti-glare slit visor

When the Crait defenses are cracked, First Order snowtroopers storm the breach and enter the darkened tunnels.

SNOWTROOPERS

Although Crait superficially resembles an ice planet, it is in fact a temperate world. The salt coating and crystalline structure have enough in common with subzero environments—intense surface glare and low skid resistance—that the First Order deploys its snowtrooper forces as infantry. The heating units that line their armor and gear are deactivated for this particular assignment.

The First Order walkers assemble in classic Veers Formation. In this attack strategy, the AT-M6s are tasked with the destruction of the enemy base's artillery defenses.

AT-ST

The First Order's scout walkers are built upon the classic All Terrain Scout Transport design, with some modest updates. Improved gyroscopic systems have stabilized the walker's balance, and the armored shell has been upgraded following new breakthroughs in lightweight materials.

Unit marking

Shin strut

Reinforced cockpit armor

Layered body armor

Cockpit entry ramp for docking (retracted)

AT-AT

Dating back to the Clone Wars, the venerable All Terrain Armored Transport has seen some upgrades for its latest First Order iteration. Lighter materials, as strong as Galactic Civil War-era armor, can now be layered, providing even more protection without increasing weight.

Directed repulsorlift recoil buffer

Comms antenna

Weight-distributing footpad

Defense turret

Armored kyber breech and fueling port

SUPERLASER SIEGE CANNON

To penetrate the Resistance defenses, the First Order airlifts a massive superlaser siege cannon to Crait's surface. Towed by tug walkers, the enormous 200-meter-long weapon is a piece of miniaturized Death Star technology. A fiery tracer beam creates a path along which a devastating pulse travels toward the target, detonating with terrifying impact. The cannon requires time to charge up between blasts, however, during which time it is vulnerable, necessitating escort walkers and air support.

Retractable stabilization outriggers

AT-HH

Pulling the siege cannon across the battlefield on ultra-dense cables are crustacean-like tug walkers, more formally identified as All Terrain Heavy Haulers, or AT-HH walkers. Their legs are a complex arrangement of crowded, redundant limbs that greatly increase the craft's resistance to battle damage.

Forcing cone barrel head

Flashback suppressor field generators

Rotating rifled collimator assembly

Bundled strand made of 27,572 steelton wires

RESISTANCE GROUND FORCES

THE RELENTLESS First Order pursuit forces the Resistance to land on Crait, and the conflict must now be decided by a surface assault. Although the Resistance has the advantage of defending a fortified position, it is hopelessly outnumbered. Every capable Resistance fighter must pick up a blaster rifle, and try to hold back the First Order long enough for a feeble distress signal to reach anyone capable of mounting a rescue. The abandoned rebel outpost's energy shield prevents orbital bombardment, while its trench network and artillery emplacements transform Crait into a formidable, if desperate, bulwark.

Trenches carved into the crystalline rock of Crait form frontline and reserve positions for infantry defenders, supported by heavy artillery pieces and anti-armor cannons. The troops can retreat back into the base through underground tunnels.

Vo-pickup

WRIST-MOUNTED COMM

GENERAL EMATT

The dwindling roster of Resistance leadership has led to Major Caluan Ematt taking on the rank of general as he organizes and leads the exterior defense of the Crait outpost. Ematt is a veteran of the Galactic Civil War, having served in the Rebel Alliance since its earliest days. He was among the first of the former rebels to answer Leia Organa's call to form the Resistance, and accompanied Leia during her recruitment of Poe Dameron. He has watched the young pilot's career with great admiration.

DATA FILE

> Image-intensifying quadnoculars employ digital filters to reduce the blinding glare of Crait's salt flats.

> The Resistance is forced to use small arms fire to hold off TIE fighter strafing runs, a desperate move that requires pinpoint accuracy.

Multi-mag tactical ammunition pouch harness

Weatherproof insulated jacket

Neuro-Saav TE4.4 field quadnoculars

BlasTech EL-16 blaster rifle

Officer's boots are soon salt encrusted

RESISTANCE TROOPS

The Resistance doesn't have dedicated infantry units. The soldiers defending Crait are technicians, pilots, and security sentries. Regular combat drills and clear lines of command prepare these improvised soldiers for the worst, and they put up a tenacious defense against the inexorable First Order advance. They retreat only when all other options have been exhausted. Many do not survive the onslaught.

Bunched collar opens up to become hood

Protective antiglare visor

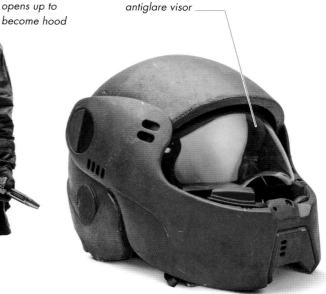

SMALL ARMS
Outdated EL-16 rifles make up the bulk of the small arms carried by the Resistance. Breaking into Crait's Rebellion-era armories, the troops power up their weapons with old rebel cartridges. As a result, their blaster bolts change color from blue to red.

BLASTECH DT-15 BLASTER PISTOL

BLASTECH EL-16HFE (HEAVY FIELD EDITION) RIFLE

Power setting adjust

SERGEANT COBEL TANSIRCH

TROOPER HELMET
Like most Resistance equipment, the helmets worn on Crait are New Republic surplus, and date back to before the mass disarmament that occurred at the end of the Galactic Civil War. No longer manufactured, these helmets came to Leia via a "misdirected" shipment from a friendly senator.

SKI SPEEDERS

Crait's discarded Rebellion-era technology includes a small number of barely functional V-4X-D ski speeders (also known as skim speeders). Rickety repulsorcraft that actually predate the Rebel Alliance, the V-4X-Ds are ultra-light low-altitude craft that employ a ventral halofoil for stabilization and maneuverability. The rebels of yesteryear outfitted these one-time civilian sporting vehicles with a light coating of armor—too much would encumber the craft—and outrigger laser cannons. During the Battle of Crait, Poe Dameron leads a frenzied defense of the entrenched Resistance with a squadron of hastily assembled ski speeders.

The speeder cockpit, nicknamed the "tub" by Resistance personnel, is open to the air, with a reinforced windshield to protect the pilot. The Rebellion did at least see fit to place extra armor along the cockpit module's nose.

NODIN CHAVDRI

Emergency flight vest

Shuttle and transport pilot livery

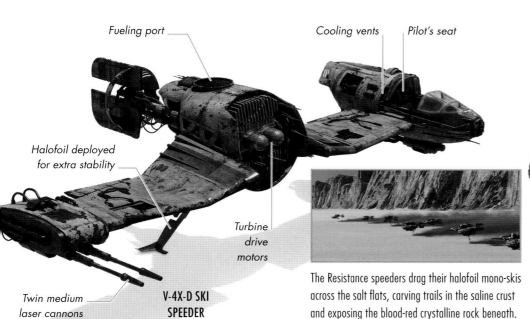

Fueling port

Cooling vents

Pilot's seat

Halofoil deployed for extra stability

Turbine drive motors

Twin medium laser cannons

V-4X-D SKI SPEEDER

The Resistance speeders drag their halofoil mono-skis across the salt flats, carving trails in the saline crust and exposing the blood-red crystalline rock beneath.

INDEX

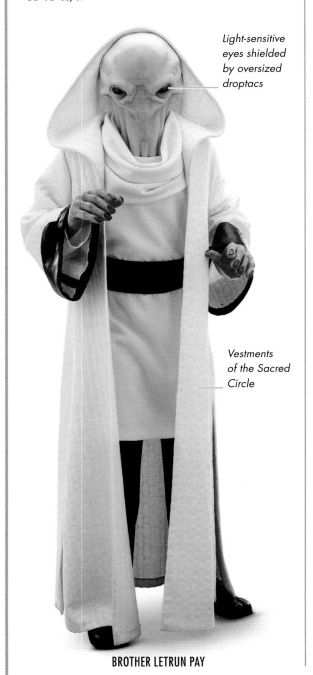

INDEX

PORTABLE TANDEM COMM-SCAN SYSTEM

Tattered combat cap

SALAKA KUCHIMBA

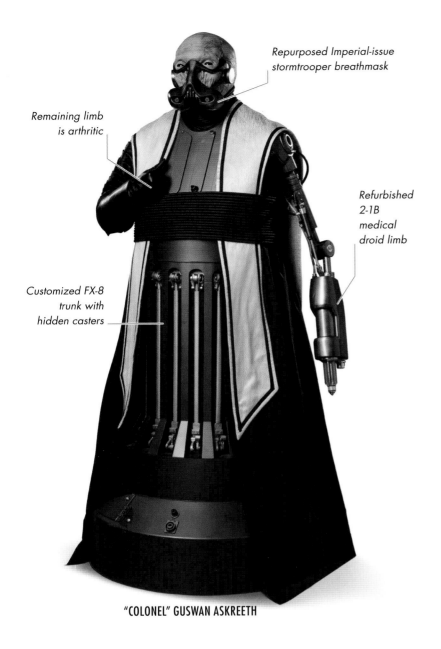

Remaining limb is arthritic

Repurposed Imperial-issue stormtrooper breathmask

Refurbished 2-1B medical droid limb

Customized FX-8 trunk with hidden casters

"COLONEL" GUSWAN ASKREETH

Senior Editor David Fentiman
Senior Designer Owen Bennett
Creative Technical Support Tom Morse and Andrew Bishop
Pre-production Producer Marc Staples
Senior Producer Mary Slater
Managing Editor Sadie Smith
Managing Art Editor Vicky Short
Publisher Julie Ferris
Art Director Lisa Lanzarini
Publishing Director Simon Beecroft

For Lucasfilm
Senior Editor Brett Rector
Asset Management Steve Newman, Newell Todd,
Gabrielle Levenson, Erik Sanchez, Bryce Pinkos, and Travis Murray
Art Director Troy Alders
Story Group James Waugh, Pablo Hidalgo,
Leland Chee, and Matt Martin
Photographers Jonathan Olley, Ed Miller, John Wilson,
Shannon Kirbie, David James, and Bruno Dayan

First American Edition, 2017
Published in the United States by DK Publishing
345 Hudson Street, New York, New York 10014

Page design copyright © 2017 Dorling Kindersley Limited
DK, a Division of Penguin Random House LLC
17 18 19 20 21 10 9 8 7 6 5 4 3 2 1
001–298143–December/2017

A catalog record for this book is available from the Library of Congress.

ISBN 978-1-4654-5551-2

DK books are available at special discounts when purchased in bulk for sales promotions, premiums,
fundraising, or educational use. For details, contact:
DK Publishing Special Markets, 345 Hudson Street, New York, New York 10014
SpecialSales@dk.com

Printed and bound in the USA

A WORLD OF IDEAS:
SEE ALL THERE IS TO KNOW
www.dk.com
www.starwars.com

ACKNOWLEDGMENTS

Pablo Hidalgo: Being enmeshed in the creation of *The Last Jedi* was an incredible highlight both professionally and, of course, personally as a lifelong *Star Wars* fan. Thank you so much to Rian Johnson and Ram Bergman for such generous access to the making of our beloved "Space Bear" adventure, and to Kiri Hart and Kathleen Kennedy for making it all possible.

Thanks to Leopold Hughes for making sure no request got lost in a very busy production schedule. Huge thanks to Neal Scanlan and crew for the tour of Canto Bight. At ILM, thank you to Ben Morris, Eddie Pasquarello, Janet Lewin, and Jack Finch for the invitations to each of the effects reviews. Also at Lucasfilm, thanks to Phil Szostak, Brian Miller, Newell Todd, Gabe Levenson, Bryce Pinkos, Erik Sanchez, and Dan Lobl for their help in tracking down reference, and to Lisa Aron and Lori Gianino for building the repository for that reference.

Thanks to fellow lore-experts Leland Chee and Matt Martin, as well as Jason Fry and Kemp Remillard. At Lucasfilm publishing, much appreciation to Michael Siglain, Sammy Holland, and Brett Rector. Writing for DK continues to be an honor, so I raise a toast to Owen Bennett, David Fentiman, and Sadie Smith.

Thank you to Kristen for everything—you got to see a real fathier run!

Oh, and to Rian and Noah, thanks for BNAT.

DK Publishing: We would like to thank Pablo Hidalgo for his dedication and professionalism, and Michael Siglain, Sammy Holland, and Brett Rector at Lucasfilm publishing for all of their hard work and assistance while this book was in production. We would also like to thank Ruth Amos, Beth Davies, Chris Gould, and Clive Savage for their superlative editorial and design assistance.